The Meaning of Life

Jules Smith

Dedication

This book is dedicated to all the wonderful people that bared their souls on these pages in a collaboration to find 'The Meaning of Life.'

Table of Contents

The Meaning of Life

It's the age old question that we all ask ourselves at least once, if not many times, in our lifetime. Why am I here? What's the point? What's the end game?

As we age and mature with experience trying to find some sort of meaning becomes paramount. Have I done anything of any magnitude or significance?

What if I haven't set the world on fire yet?

Because of this often asked but unanswered question, I decided to try and find out 'The Meaning of Life' by asking 100 people a set of 9 formulated, deep and meaningful questions. Collaboration usually brings about an answer and I remembered a story I'd heard that took place at a country fair. Everyone who attended was asked to guess the weight of the resident bull in the field. Not one single person got the correct answer but when the combination of guessed weights were added together and divided by the amount of people who took part, the bull's weight was absolutely spot on. I came to the conclusion that if I asked 100 people a set of questions and analysed the data thereafter, some sort of meaning would make itself evident and we could all sleep at night.

The Participants

The people who kindly took part in my project are from all walks of life and an even split between male and female. They are all aged over 30 in order to have enough worldly experience to give constructive answers to the posed questions. Some have remained anonymous using a pseudonym for privacy purposes and others have used their real names.

The Questions

I chose a set of 9 questions that would make people stop and think seriously about life: what they had done so far, how they might have changed their past, or not, whether faith played a part, and all the good, the bad, and the ugly parts of life. All of these questions were set out in an order to bring about a range of emotions: self awareness, self analysis, humility, pride, and so forth. All leading to the ultimate and final question, "What is the Meaning of life?"

Here are the questions below with my reasons for asking each particular one.

Do you believe in God?

Faith is a big one and can shape how an individual looks at life and the way they deal with the ups and downs of their journey. I wanted to find out if belief and hope made a significant difference to a person's outlook and their ability to look at experiences, particularly unpleasant ones, with a more positive slant and whether having faith resulted in a more confident approach and outlook to life.

What is the worst thing you've ever done?

We have all done something bad, either off the scale or just minor, but all of us feel ashamed of something we have done. We all like to believe we are good people though we have all erred in some way. As a race we are quick to judge, often forgetting we too have caused stress or pain to somebody else at some time despite where we might be now. I asked this question as it makes a person look at the flawed version of themselves and get in touch with humility.

What is your greatest achievement?

This question gave people a chance to share something they felt good about achieving even though most people don't think they've done anything outstanding. We all want to boast about something to prove our worthiness to others and at the same time feel bad about doing so due to how we have been brought up: Nobody likes a braggart. I wanted people to get in touch with pride and reveal something that they felt was a personal accomplishment.

Tell me a secret about you

First of all, it's no longer a secret if you have to tell me! Some people clocked onto that straightaway! That also means they are not comfortable in releasing that information to me or the world. Most people tend to think of something dark and nefarious that they might have done when first asked this question even though a secret can be something good. Things we keep secret tend to be that which we believe we are going to be judged on by others. Much like question 2, it gets people reaching deep within and more likely to open up to their feelings and awareness of right and wrong.

If you could go back in time to age 20 with your current life experience, what would you do differently?

Hindsight. What a wonderful thing. How many times have you said to yourself, "If I knew back then what I know now…"

Given the chance, what would you change?

There is a 15 year old standing in front of you. What life advice would you give him/her?

This question is much like the above, however, what we have done and what we might advise another to do can be quite different. The participants in this book have made mistakes but may also have not taken the risks they thought they should have. What people actually do as opposed to what they think they should do can be poles apart. Advice from the experienced and wise!

When you are an elderly person, sitting in your rocking chair and you look back on your life, what do you want to have achieved?

This is quite a hard hitting question, particularly for those of us who fear time is running out and we haven't yet done all the things we thought we should have. This question makes a person think about what is really important and cut out the background noise that fills in the gaps. At the end of it all, what is it you want to see left behind you?

Give me one word that sums up your life journey thus far:

I wanted people to sum up their life to date in one word and whether that word had a positive or negative outlook.

What is the meaning of life?

After answering all the questions above regarding achievements, failings, secrets, hindsight, and the trail left behind, I felt that each person would be in the best frame of mind to answer this important question with heartfelt honesty.

I would like to thank all the people who kindly participated in this experience. Some found the questions very difficult, some people cried, but on the whole most found the experience to be very cathartic and useful. I hope you, the reader, enjoy their answers and sound advice. I believe this is one of the greatest and most honest self help books available!

At the end of the book I have analysed the answers leaving you with the "The Meaning of Life" and perhaps, the very meaning in it too.

Participants

Name: Charlie Big Potatoes

Age: 65

Gender: Male

Country: England

Occupation: Social Lubricant

Do you believe in God?

After a chequered and torturous past, yes. Having attended church from Sunday school to being best man at 14 weddings, I always considered church services and sermons as akin to dishing out a personal bollocking. It was only after losing my only (brief) marriage at the age of 49 and simultaneously losing my home, job and finances, I turned to God. Despite serving as a lay reader for a time, I don't particularly enjoy 'High Church' as it's too ritualistic and resembles a choreographed process which excludes the uninitiated in church services. I did enjoy the Pentecostal 'happy clappy' experience; far more inclusive and jolly. I now pray daily in the shower, rather than wanking. But I also find myself lobbing silent prayers to complete strangers on my travels, like a spiritual Frisbee. I pray for the homeless person huddled under wet cardboard in a shop doorway, the beggar on a piss-stained pavement, the forlorn Big Issue seller, the struggling anxious faced parent, the confused crying child. No one knows I'm praying for them but my prayers are sent with a message of love, hope happiness and blessings. In the walk of life, my prayers might seem insignificant but as someone wiser than me said, "It is the greatest of all mistakes to do nothing because you can only do a little – do what you can".

What is the worst thing you've ever done?

I can't think of a sin or crime I haven't committed. With age comes a conscience, which in my case gets larger with age. They say emotional baggage never gets lost in transit. That's really fucking true. Perhaps the worst thing I've ever done is getting my first girlfriend pregnant. We were too young to consider anything other than an abortion and I was too arrogant to consider any inconvenience to my hedonistic attitude. I suppose that makes me a murderer. I pray for that lost soul every day and I remain thoroughly ashamed of myself.

What is your greatest achievement?

I would say it's still being alive. I've smoked heavily since I was 14. I went through a ten year phase of drinking a bottle of vodka and two bottles of wine a day. From the ages of 20 to 30, I wished only for a ten year period of utter self indulgence and self absorbed fun. It became a genuine shock to still be alive on my 30th birthday. So much so, I undertook a kaleidoscopic journey of mental breakdowns, a lamentable suicide attempt and a veritable raft of assorted therapies. Only the faded scars on my wrists indicate my greatest achievement of still being alive.

Tell me a secret about you:

I have only ever been truly faithful to two things in my life: supporting Millwall football club and smoking. My early home life was hell. It was physically, emotionally and verbally violent. I was always told I was "as thick as shit". If I had received a penny for every time I was told by my parents that they'd "wished they had drowned me at birth", I wouldn't have undertaken so much thieving and skulduggery. No one could hate me more than I hated myself and my life. On a positive note, thanks to therapy and time, I now have a very good relationship with my mum and I pray that my dad is safe and blessed in heaven.

If you could go back in time to age 20 with your current life experience, what would you do differently?

Therapists say "Show me the child of seven and I'll show you the adult". I would have started therapy straight away. I wasted years as an emotional nomad, lost in a loveless wilderness. I probably would not have smoked. On the other hand, I like a smoke.

There is a 15 year old standing in front of you. What life advice would you give him/her?

Someone somewhere loves you. You are a child of God and the universe. You are unique. You deserve a good life. Be kind. Be a magpie, a sponge, in terms of seeking and absorbing every facet of life. Even if you don't believe this, difficult as it might be, try not to be a twat.

When you are an elderly person, sitting in your rocking chair and you look back on your life, what do you want to have achieved?

Only one thing: I never want my fifteen year-old son to look over his shoulder in his life and wonder if he was loved.

Give me one word that sums up your life journey thus far: Emotional

What is the meaning of life?

Do no harm to others. We can't do much about the life we are given but we can do something about the person we're growing into. Every day we have a choice on how we treat ourselves and other people. We can choose to be a curmudgeon or a kindness. Never underestimate the effect one has on other people.

I left school aged fifteen without any qualifications. After a series of jobs, I joined the NHS in 1976. I started as a cleaner, porter, administrator and 16 years later became a human resources director. I gained a diploma in human resources management. During my NHS service I was a branch secretary of a major trade union and a senior member of the Trade Union Council. In 1995 at the age of

50 I gave up my well paid NHS job, performance related pay, and lease car. I did a three year honours degree in arts and humanities for performing arts. In 1998 I graduated with a 2.1 upper division honours degree.

Name: Angie

Age: 41

Gender: Female

Country: USA

Occupation: Upper level office dweller (sales, support, consulting, technology)

Do you believe in God?

If you'd asked me this when I was 20 I'd have given a resounding yes. These days I am less and less sure. I see so much heartbreak in the world. It seems unfathomable that the God I used to believe in would allow such things to happen.

What is the worst thing you've ever done?

I accepted a marriage proposal I knew I couldn't actually commit to because I didn't want to deal with the look of pain on his face staring at me from across the table. I called later to say I couldn't accept, but he had already told his family and friends.

What is your greatest achievement?

It's going to seem cliché, but my kids are truly the greatest thing I've ever done. Being a single mom is a real pain in the ass sometimes. It's lonely and stressful more often than not. Still, I have raised two very respectful and intelligent kids with wicked senses of humor.

Tell me a secret about you:

At 41 years old I am still waiting for the moment when I'll feel like I'm enough. Each year I am a bit more accepting of myself, but there is more to come.

If you could go back in time to age 20 with your current life experience, what would you do differently?

College before 30. There are a lot of ways life could have been more comfortable if I had knocked out college before my kids were starting school.

There is a 15 year old standing in front of you. What life advice would you give him/her?

It seems like these friends of yours are the end all be all of your world. Chances are, most of them won't be in your life past high school. Don't let people who do not have a long term investment in your life dictate your actions. Be you. Screw the peer pressure. You're becoming you forever. They are your friends only for as long as they choose.

When you are an elderly person, sitting in your rocking chair and you look back on your life, what do you want to have achieved?

I would like to have set foot on all continents. It's not a huge dream in the grand scheme of things.

Give me one word that sums up your life journey thus far: Detours

What is the meaning of life?

If by definition you mean, what does it mean to live… Then the meaning of life is to become an active and present part of the world around you, while putting more positive into the world than negative. If you meant what is the ultimate goal… then I would have to say finding serenity and peace with yourself.

Given the post-30 ages of the respondents, I'd love to know what their biggest regrets are. For me, it is that I should have learned French and moved to Montreal years ago. There was possibility there once that could have been amazing and beautiful.

Name: Alex

Age: 44

Gender: Male

Country: Lithuania

Occupation: President of Alterations Studio

Do you believe in God?

Not really.

What is the worst thing you've ever done?

Punched a younger teen for nothing and drown the cat.

What is your greatest achievement?

Basketball team captain.

Tell me a secret about you:

I am an alcoholic, I think.

If you could go back in time to age 20 with your current life experience, what would you do differently?

Nothing.

There is a 15-year-old standing in front of you. What life advice would you give him/her?

Alex says relax!

When you are an elderly person, sitting in your rocking chair and you look back on your life, what do you want to have achieved?

Money rules the world.

Give me one word that sums up your life journey thus far: Passion

What is the meaning of life?

Enjoy, if you can...

Name: Annie P Holmes

Age: 60

Gender: Female

Country: England

Occupation: Retired

Do you believe in God?

The $64,000 question! Do I believe in an old, bearded man, who resides somewhere up in the clouds looking down on humanity, moving us around like chess pieces and answering some people's prayers, and ignoring others? Absolutely not. Do I believe in the angry, spiteful, vengeful, petulant creature that features so heavily in the old testament (I should because I was raised a Catholic); the one that sends us to Hell if we don't obey and worship him properly? The one that watches people slaughter each other in wars? The one that makes sure we have enough disease, poverty and famine to keep us struggling millennia after millennia? No, no and no! The very notion of such an entity is anathema to me; an utterly insane and nonsensical idea, and I don't understand how millions of seemingly otherwise intelligent people buy into it. Really and truly you might just as well follow the Sugar Plum Fairy or Rumplestiltskin!

But what I do believe is this; the universe is an impossibly vast and mysterious place and we are only just beginning to understand how some of the strange stuff out there works. Everything comes down to physics and mathematics and everything behaves in particular ways and follows certain "rules". How and why is it like that I wonder? Our universe started with an almighty explosion, but what caused that explosion and what was there before it happened? Then there's energy - it cannot be created or destroyed; it is eternal! I mean wow! Think about the implications of that! For instance, I would understand that to mean when we die our energy is transformed or transferred to another form. It is conserved. And then you've got Dark Matter. That stuff that makes up 80% of the universe; the material that we can't see in between all the stuff that we can see! What is it? Where did it come from and what does it do?

If there is a god, then it is a thing that is so huge and so complex that it bears no resemblance to the mythological fiend in various books. Einstein used the word "god" as a shorthand for the laws of physics and I really like that. I do think that there is Something that drives the universe and binds it all together somehow, and I think one day science and mathematics and physics will give us the answers.

What is the worst thing you've ever done?

1. When I was about 7 and my sister was about 4 I took her on a "magical mystery tour" of the back garden. I blindfolded her and told her I was going to take her to a magic place where there were fairies. Instead I led her to a patch of stinging nettles and sat her down in them! It stung her badly and she ran to mum screaming and crying. It was a horrible thing to do, and I rightly got into trouble. I adore my younger sister and have no idea why I would even think about that, let alone do it! But at the time I thought it was funny and got a warped sense of satisfaction out of it. I wonder if all small children have occasional and temporary streaks of cruelty and nastiness in them?

2. About 25 years ago when I was still working I went out on a lunch-break with two friends. Friend A was driving and Friend B was in the front seat and I was in the back. When we came back from lunch we parked next to Friend B's much loved little sports car. To my utter horror the wind snatched my door as I climbed out and whacked it into the back panel of said little sports car leaving a horrid ugly dent and a scratch. Neither of my friends noticed what had happened and, completely out of character for me, I shut the back door and said nothing! The next day Friend B was telling me about the awful mark she'd found on her car and was very upset and tearful about it., wondering how it had happened and who did it. I sympathised with her but still did not own up to being the culprit!! All these years later I still feel very

ashamed and guilty about what I did, and felt so rotten I haven't lied or concealed anything since.

What is your greatest achievement?

Well, I never swam the channel, climbed Everest or trekked the Sahara; I never had children and my one marriage ended in divorce in 1983 after only 4 years so I'm struggling a bit with this one. I would say, however, that I have lived in my current home for 35 years and in that time I have created a sanctuary, making it into a warm, cosy, peaceful and welcoming haven. It is a special place and everyone loves it here, and when we've all had periods of turmoil and various ups and downs, this little house of mine has been the one constant in all our lives, providing a refuge and bolt hole for various friends and family whenever they've needed it.

Tell me a secret about you:

Four years ago I drove down to a hotel in Sussex and had sex with a very gorgeous, very sexy young man 28 years younger than me after chatting on a "cougar" website!!!! Hahahahahahaha - it was good!

If you could go back in time to age 20 with your current life experience, what would you do differently?

Oh god, everything! I would not marry my ex-husband as I think I probably made him very unhappy and ended up divorcing him. He loved me completely and he really didn't deserve me or what I did to him. I would not date most of the men I dated as I always made really poor and stupid choices and they ended up making me very miserable. It probably served me right for making my poor husband so miserable! I would not do the jobs I did as I hated them all! I left school in 1974 with no clear idea of what I wanted to do (other than go to drama school but my parents could not afford to send me), and so my dad made me go into office work as I had learnt typing at school, but I went from one office job to another completely dissatisfied and unfulfilled.

There is a 15 year old standing in front of you. What life advice would you give him/her?

"Annie, PLEASE DO NOT go out with James Davies! You will utterly waste three very valuable and precious years with him and he will make you terribly unhappy and screw you up beyond belief! He will damage your psyche beyond repair, and you will never trust men again. There is not one single good thing that will come out of this relationship. For the love of god girl concentrate on your studies, and your writing and painting - PLEASE don't let this talent go! And be determined about going to drama school. Even though mum and dad can't afford to send you, do your very best to get there yourself!"

When you are an elderly person, sitting in your rocking chair and you look back on your life, what do you want to have achieved?

Not much really. I have no great plans, dreams or ambitions and no unattainable goals. I just want to have had as peaceful and stress-free a life as possible, and to have been as contented as I could be. Given that life can be such a bloody bitch at times, that in itself promises to be quite a tall order! I want to be a memorable and eccentric great aunt to my two great nieces, and I want to have succeeded in being/becoming the best version of me that I could be. Also, given that I have Crohn's disease and it has almost killed me twice, if I can get through the rest of my life relatively unscathed and pain free I will have achieved more than I could hope for!

Give me one word that sums up your life journey thus far: Growth

What is the meaning of life?

Oooh the biggest question of all!

On the one hand I don't think there IS a meaning of life. It's all just physics, chemistry, science and mathematics as a result of the big bang. It's just a constant process of evolution in a continually expanding universe, and to that extent MY life has no extra special meaning or purpose any more than, say, the life of my cats, or my plants and my trees.

On the other hand, when you consider how this planet is positioned exactly just so within our solar system that life was able to start here at all; that we have a wonderful and delicately complex eco system that is perfectly balanced to continue that life, and that everything, absolutely EVERYTHING is linked, related, interconnected and intertwined, then the meaning of life for me Has to be that we are all just a little piece of an unimaginably huge and eternal picture that only physics and science (god) can eventually explain and reveal.

Hey! Everyone! Stop craving useless and stupid shit!!

Name: Andrew Peter Cass

Age: 63

Gender: Straight male

Country: England

Occupation: Picture Framer - Proprietor

Do you believe in God?

Biblical God, no. Infinite God we cannot comprehend, yes.

What is the worst thing you've ever done?

Drink driving. I could have killed someone.

What is your greatest achievement?

No great achievements just hundreds of satisfying ones.

Tell me a secret about you:

I've kissed a man.

If you could go back in time to age 20 with your current life experience, what would you do differently?

Had kids. I'd have made a great dad.

There is a 15 year old standing in front of you. What life advice would you give him/her?

Never take drugs and be honest to yourself and others.

When you are an elderly person, sitting in your rocking chair and you look back on your life, what do you want to have achieved?

Just the satisfaction that I have lead a good, happy and enjoyable life.

Give me one word that sums up your life journey thus far: Satisfying

What is the meaning of life?

Who knows? Life seems so diverse in all walks to really mean anything. Prolog: If God is alive and well he will be working on a less ambitious project, and in the words of writer Arthur. C.Clarke, "It may be that our role on this planet is not to worship God but to create him."

Name: Char

Age: 44

Gender: Female

Country: UK

Occupation: Finance director that doesn't get fucking paid.

Do you believe in God?

I would like to think that I believed in him, however if there was a God he's giving us a pretty shitty deal. I've suffered some losses, deaths of people close to me at an early age which I struggled to come to terms with. I'm very unsure what my beliefs are.

What is the worst thing you've ever done?

My biggest regret is leaving Canada and that became a real issue when I turned 40 and realised I'd left an opportunity over there. I miss the lifestyle, the scenery, location. I enjoy travel. I want to retire at 50 and rent accommodation in various places in the USA and Canada for 6 months of the year.

What is your greatest achievement?

My children.

Tell me a secret about you:

I've saved three peoples lives: One from drowning in Canada. We were on a house boat and my friend fell overboard and hit her head and got knocked unconscious. I jumped in and got her out. I was on the school run and a boy ran out behind a bus into oncoming traffic. I jumped out in front of the car clipped me causing bruising, the boy got away. The third one: We had friends visiting from Vancouver. I cooked a lovely roast beef dinner which one of guests choked on and I had to give him the Heimlich manoeuvre! He was 6'4″ but I picked him up like he was weightless. He threw up the roast beef and then sat back down and carried on eating. I however, needed another drink from shock.

If you could go back in time to age 20 with your current life experience, what would you do differently?

I would not have left Canada. I wouldn't have started smoking. I would have had a little bit more time and patience with my Nan. She was a pain in the arse but now she's not here I wish I'd have given her more time. I wouldn't have sold my spitfire for £500 but that was my one way ticket to Vancouver. I think knowing what I know now at 20, I would have invested my money better and developed my property portfolio more. One of the best things that happened to me on life's travels was meeting my good friend Juliette, so I wouldn't change that, thank you.

There is a 15 year old standing in front of you. What life advice would you give him/her?

Embrace your education. Develop your social skills which means interacting with your peers and adults. Follow your dreams. Persevere. There are going to be rough times; rough and smooth, but stay focussed on your future and your dreams and ambitions.

When you are an elderly person, sitting in your rocking chair and you look back on your life, what do you want to have achieved?

I want to achieve the plans and the things I'm putting in place now. I want to look back and think " Yeah, Char, You did everything you set out to do." You spend an awful lot of time making plans but life in gets in the way; obstacles and distractions. Everything I write down on my lists, I want to achieve.

Give me one word that sums up your life journey thus far: Adventurous

What is the meaning of life?

To love, laugh and be happy.

I'm very humbled and privileged to have married the love of my life.

Is the interview over now? OK, let's have another tequila sunrise.

Name: AJ

Age: 49

Gender: Male

Country: UK

Occupation: Head of Recruitment

Do you believe in God?

No – because even though I see incredible things every day I am not convinced that it was all created by a single being. So who created it in the first place? I don't know. If HE exists who created God?

What is the worst thing you've ever done?

My greatest regret and worst decision was the termination of my third child. Although the reasoning seemed sound at the time it is something I have never got past or forgiven myself for.

What is your greatest achievement?

Despite my numerous flaws I have managed to create an environment where my children have grown up unafraid to express themselves with strong individual personalities and the ability to form strong, relevant and well informed views. They are incredible people with such potential and most importantly to me are loved by their peers because they are neither cruel nor mean. I did not do this alone by any means.

Tell me a secret about you:

I work with people in a customer facing role which requires me to interact at a very involved level with many different people. The secret is that I actually don't like interacting with people. I prefer to be alone or with my close family. I only have 1 friend that I spend time with regularly. When you interact with me I am the life and soul, the reality is I'm quite boring.

If you could go back in time to age 20 with your current life experience, what would you do differently?

Go into property sooner and stay there. Go and find my wife 4 years earlier and enjoy 4 more fabulous years. Have a green Mohican just once! Listen.

There is a 15 year old standing in front of you. What life advice would you give him/her?

Harness the fire within you, don't let it consume you. Listen to those who know better and don't just up and leave when you don't like what is being said. You can't start by running the company, but if you follow the process you will in time. When you find her, treat her well and no matter what never do anything stupid enough to lose her because you will never replace the one. Don't stand on the side-lines watching, get in and have a go, you might just enjoy yourself. Providing you aren't harming them, other peoples thoughts on how silly you look, really don't matter.

When you are an elderly person, sitting in your rocking chair and you look back on your life, what do you want to have achieved?

Happiness. I want to see my children and their children living full and complicated lives, being challenged and tested and really living this thing we call life. I want to be able to help them through should they need me. I want to have many fantastic memories to laugh with my wife about and to remember the fabulous things that we've done, however mundane those things may appear to others. I want to have been the best that I can be.

Give me one word that sums up your life journey thus far: Breathtaking

What is the meaning of life?

It is simply to fill whatever time you have with as many wonderful things as you can. Be they sights, smells, activities or perfect moments, the memories are what you take with you. Most importantly to me, the meaning of life is that it is shared with one that you love more than yourself. An experience that is experienced alone might as well not have happened, the memory is kept alive by sharing. Your greatest gift both given and received is love.

Take more time to reflect on your life, this exercise has made me cry.

Name: Crystal Collier

Age: 37

Gender: Female

Country: USA

Occupation: Mother/Author/Musician/Home School Teacher

Do you believe in God?

Like I believe in the sun.

What is the worst thing you've ever done?

Steal and lie about it. Ah, childhood…

What is your greatest achievement?

My children. All five of them.

Tell me a secret about you:

I constantly listen to orchestras in my head that have never been written, so much so that listening to radio or CD's often agitates me.

If you could go back in time to age 20 with your current life experience, what would you do differently?

Have more patience. LOL. Truthfully, I'd put more into savings and force my husband to deal with a higher level of organization. ;)

There is a 15 year old standing in front of you. What life advice would you give him/her?

It's not all about you. This stage of life is difficult. You're learning who you are, and a huge part of that is exploration. However, you will learn the most about who you are when you forget yourself and focus on others. Not only will you discover the things that make you awesome, you'll discover the greatest and most lasting happiness. When you focus inward, you shrink. When you focus outward, you expand. Be a star. And what do stars do? : Sustain life for others and produce life-building elements with which planets are formed. You have the power inside to build worlds.

When you are an elderly person, sitting in your rocking chair and you look back on your life, what do you want to have achieved?

I want to have made a difference in the world, but not the loud, write-my-name-in-lights kind of difference. I hope my legacy will be felt wherever my children, grandchildren, and great grandchildren go, through the love and kindness they spread. If I'm lucky enough to personally touch a few hearts along the way or encourage a couple despondent souls, I'll be fulfilled.

Give me one word that sums up your life journey thus far: Intense

What is the meaning of life?

To become. If you believe in an afterlife, you have to believe you enter that sphere with the same desires and appetites with which you left this one. Every daily choice is forming your character. Either you are constantly becoming a better person, or a worse one. And yes, we oscillate up and down, and that's okay, as long as we are angled the right direction. It's like climbing a mountain. We are not meant to reach a single peek and call it good. We're meant to climb and build strength, constantly reaching for the next high point. Who do you want to be when this life is done? Do you want to be able to look back and feel a sense of satisfaction with your accomplishments? Every day is another opportunity to build your eternal character. Don't waste a single one.

Name: Art inc.

Age: 43

Gender: Male.

Country: England

Occupation: Artist

Do you believe in God?

I've never really believed in a god. I can't see any comfort in doing so and I don't feel like anything is missing from my life. There have been thousands of deities over the history of humankind, yet people only choose to believe in a god they have been indoctrinated with, its convenient that isn't it. There is ample evidence to convince me that homo sapiens have been around longer than the idea of any god has. People tend to cherry pick the nice bits about god and religion, and ignore the bits they don't like. It certainly has no place in the governing of any society.

I enjoy watching the videos of Christopher Hitchen's and Sam Harris, where they argue against the existence of god. They put it much better than I ever could.

I would take no comfort from believing I was going to live eternally in some kind of an afterlife. In my opinion, living your life without bowing down to any deity, then simply switching off when you die is fine. Why does there have to be anything after that. I'm not aware of anything when I am asleep, and for that reason I am not afraid of death. I'm not saying I am not afraid of the process of dying, but everyone has to experience that whether they are religious or not, however I am convinced that when I am gone then that is it, goodnight Vienna!

What is the worst thing you've ever done?

I'm not sure I have any regrets. You do what you think is right at the time. If it turns out to be a mistake then you still learn something which may help next time. I wish I had spent more time with certain people that aren't here any more. I'm not one for dwelling on the past so I don't really think about it. If I do then it tends to be the good times I remember.

What is your greatest achievement?

Creating art that other people deem good enough to spend their hard earned money on.

Tell me a secret about you:

Despite having ideals close to pacifism, I love guns and knives, although I'm very eager to assert that I have never hurt a living creature with either of them.

If you could go back in time to age 20 with your current life experience, what would you do differently?

I would have followed my heart and become an artist / art dealer, instead of beginning later in life like I have done.

There is a 15 year old standing in front of you. What life advice would you give him/her?

Try to treat other folks in a way that you would expect to be treated, if not better. Follow your heart and do something with your life that that you enjoy, rather than simply providing the means to exist. Cherish the company of people, or animals, that you will miss dearly when they are no longer here.

When you are an elderly person, sitting in your rocking chair and you look back on your life, what do you want to have achieved?

Happiness is all you need to achieve. Some people are unfortunate in the fact that they need much more to be happy than others do. Being creative makes me happy, so I hope I have been a creative person.

Give me one word that sums up your life journey thus far: Eclectic

What is the meaning of life?

There isn't one, and there doesn't have to be one. We find ourselves here through a serendipitous chain of events, born from a dynamic universe. We don't understand everything yet, but I'm sure we will eventually, although I doubt when we do it will provide any reason. As sentient beings we create our own meaning. It isn't my place to decide anyone else's reason to be, and I expect the same in return. If more people respected the beliefs of others, rather than trying to indoctrinate or change them, the world would be a more peaceful place to exist in. All we have is the present moment, which we should try to enjoy.

Name: Daisy Diary

Age: 50

Gender: Female

Country: UK

Occupation: Housewife

Do you believe in God?

Yes, very strongly. However, I believe that fair treatment of others and being kind is more important than going to church.

What is the worst thing you've ever done?

Boiling all the eggs before a cooking lesson at school. I never owned up.

What is your greatest achievement?

Having two amazing, talented, clever and independent children.

Tell me a secret about you:

I made love in a swimming pool with my lover while my husband and his wife were asleep on the poolside.

If you could go back in time to age 20 with your current life experience, what would you do differently?

I would be more relaxed, especially about relationships, and I'd live more.

There is a 15 year old standing in front of you. What life advice would you give him/her?

Work hard, play hard.

When you are an elderly person, sitting in your rocking chair and you look back on your life, what do you want to have achieved?

A beautiful family, loving friends, and not to have upset too many people.

Give me one word that sums up your life journey thus far: Amazing

What is the meaning of life?

Celebration! And at the end of it to have written on my headstone, "Oh no! What have I done?"

Name: Anthony Cherubino

Age: 50

Gender: Male

Country: USA

Occupation: Freelance Artist @ "The Art of an Image" (Primary Medium is Photography)

Do you believe in God?

I do. The presence of God in my life is something I simply couldn't imagine not being there. Even at the lowest points in my life, my faith has carried me.

What is the worst thing you've ever done?

I regret not furthering my education sooner.

What is your greatest achievement?

After several years of working as a substitute teacher, a former student told me I was an inspiration to stay in school and graduate. Not too bad at all.

Tell me a secret about you:

I have a gift for memorization.

If you could go back in time to age 20 with your current life experience, what would you do differently?

I got accepted to Art School and didn't go. I've always wished I had gone.

There is a 15 year old standing in front of you. What life advice would you give him/her?

Blaming others for your failures is as useless as taking credit for the success of others. Your life is your own – so own it.

When you are an elderly person, sitting in your rocking chair and you look back on your life, what do you want to have achieved?

I'd like to know that I said and did things in my life that had a positive influence and impact on others.

Give me one word that sums up your life journey thus far: Seeking

What is the meaning of life?

While it may sound jaded or even a cliché to some; I really do believe life itself is about living…taking notice of things – the good and the bad, and realizing everything has its place. If you can make something bad better – do so! Leave things better than they were when you got here if you can. Doesn't have to be much more complicated than that.

Mark Andrews from A2K photography

Name: Adele Smith

Age: 34

Gender: Female

Country: England, UK

Occupation: Vocalist

Do you believe in God?

Not in the common sense. I don't believe there is an almighty being that created nor governs us, but rather I believe in the force and will of nature. I don't think there is an afterlife waiting for us, which is why I try to make the most of everyday. We are not entitled to anything, the world owes us nothing.

What is the worst thing you've ever done?

Broken the trust someone put in me. I was young and at the time didn't realise that broken trust is something that is never truly repaired. Once someone's view of you is changed, I don't think it can ever be undone. As a friend once said to me, trust is like glass, once broken, it may be stuck back together but will never be the same. Now I am much older, I value someone's trust very highly. Live and learn!

What is your greatest achievement?

During my days as a competitive rower, I came 2nd out of 5 at race. Being shorter and a little fatter than my club-mates, I had to work really hard to do that. That was one of my two great achievements. The other was getting my ABRSM grade 5 music theory certificate. I have a degree in music, but I had to work really hard on music theory. Gawd, it was like teaching a dog to cook an omelette! I cannot imagine that these are particularly impressive, but they are my greatest because these are the things I really had to work to achieve.

Tell me a secret about you:

I really like the smell of old, dusty books.

If you could go back in time to age 20 with your current life experience, what would you do differently?

I would not blame myself for the actions of others. My father leaving was not my fault, despite what my mother tried to make me believe. I would not seek solace in alcohol and empty liaisons. I would not self harm. But then, if I not lived through this, I would not be the person I am today. So in all honesty, I would not change anything.

There is a 15 year old standing in front of you. What life advice would you give him/her?

Do not let anyone make you feel bad. They behave they way they do because they do not want to believe the truth. Their lack of perspective is not your fault. Bullies behave so because they do not know how to process primal drives or reactions to other events. But either way, it is not responsibility to save everyone. Not everyone wants to be saved. Work on your own strength before trying to reach others. This will take you 15 years to acquire and understand.

When you are an elderly person, sitting in your rocking chair and you look back on your life, what do you want to have achieved?

I want to have known the meaning of selfless love.

Give me one word that sums up your life journey thus far: AHHHHHHHHHHH!!

What is the meaning of life?

To love, be happy and care for those around you. I do not believe there is a divine purpose nor an afterlife. This is all we have. Make it count.

Name: Baz Francis Duarte

Age: 37

Gender: Cis Male

Country: USA

Occupation: Musician

Do you believe in God?

I believe in God, I just don't believe in religion.

What is the worst thing you've ever done?

I used to be a lot more aggressive as a person, both physically and verbally, and I'm not proud of how I treated some people in the past when I was like that. Once I calmed down as a person I noticed that aggression in others and became ashamed that I was once a part of that problem. The only benefit to that now is when I see someone fucking up I'm less judgemental as I often think that I would have acted or did act the same way in the past.

What is your greatest achievement?

It's musical stuff, but I don't want to blow smoke up my own arse.

Tell me a secret about you:

I am a magnet for stalkers. I have been for awhile now because I talk to strangers a lot, my Mum is the same, but when I got to a certain age I started to experience a few things that went beyond funny or cute. I have such an empathy for lonely people as I have often felt like one of them, but some people are sadly no longer reachable as good company for others. Who knows, maybe I still have more in common with them than I first thought.

If you could go back in time to age 20 with your current life experience, what would you do differently?

Act less like my tormentors.

There is a 15 year old standing in front of you. What life advice would you give him/her?

Always do what you feel is right, but don't be afraid to accept that you might be wrong.

When you are an elderly person, sitting in your rocking chair and you look back on your life, what do you want to have achieved?

More of the same, please.

Give me one word that sums up your life journey thus far: Obstinate

What is the meaning of life?

To enjoy it at no harmful cost to others.

Name: Aimée D

Age: 40

Gender: Female

Country: American by birth, lived in Germany for 14 years

Occupation: I design EFL curriculum for schools and businesses

Do you believe in God?

Church god, no… a unifying energy, oh yes! And as to the why… because I've felt it often. Particularly during the births of my two youngest children and while watching people who I dearly love pass on. These amazing fleeting moments of deep connection sustain me in dark times and keep me humble. That's the religion I choose to follow.

What is the worst thing you've ever done?

I've lied {there have been a couple of doozies} and cheated and been mean, I stole an outfit when I was 14… but the worst, the thing that makes my stomach flip flop, is when I think about times I tried to be someone I'm not… moments of impatient eye-rolling and unabashed snobbery. Especially the moments when I've acted so ridiculously in front of my kids.

What is your greatest achievement?

Moving to a new country without speaking the language or knowing anyone and (after a few embarrassing & challenging years) thriving. It is quite a feeling to be secure in knowing that no matter what or where, I'll be just fine. And besides that, quitting smoking.

Tell me a secret about you:

I'm getting ready to spend a school year in America with my kids… something I have been looking forward to for many years… But secretly I am totally nervous about fitting in Stateside. (Despite my answer to your previous question). I'm also starting a blog to keep a record of our experiences and totally surprised myself at feeling terrified at the prospect of putting myself out there. I'd really thought that I was over caring about what others think!

If you could go back in time to age 20 with your current life experience, what would you do differently?

Travel more, worry exponentially less about pleasing anyone but myself.

There is a 15 year old standing in front of you. What life advice would you give him/her?

Learn as much as you can about as much as you can… learn a skill that you can use anywhere in the world and then go… anywhere, everywhere… take chances, kiss a lot, don't take anything but your intuition so seriously. And send me postcards!!!

When you are an elderly person, sitting in your rocking chair and you look back on your life, what do you want to have achieved?

I don't know yet. There's a kind of contentment that happens when you follow your heart. I want that for sure… just not clear on the details.

Give me one word that sums up your life journey thus far: Magical

What is the meaning of life?

Doing all that you can from where you are to feel content… believing in beauty and truth, even if there's no sign of either on the horizon. And the grace to accept everyone else's same right to discovering meaning in their lives.

Name: Callum McClean

Age: 61

Gender: Male

Country: UK

Occupation: Hospital discharge assessor NHS/ semi retired

Do you believe in God?

Simple answer is no.

What is the worst thing you've ever done?

Tried to please too many people in my earlier years. Being who I thought they would want me to be instead of just being myself.

What is your greatest achievement?

I don't have a "Greatest" achievement. To live my life with a positive attitude and help those that need supporting along the way. Living and breathing every day is an achievement.

Tell me a secret about you:

If I did it would no longer be a secret, but I will tell you something that not many people know. I lost my life in a car crash April 1977. I experienced what happens after shut down. I was resuscitated by the ambulance crew. Based on this experience I now have no fear about death.

If you could go back in time to age 20 with your current life experience, what would you do differently?

I was 20 years of age when I was in the car crash. If I knew now what I knew then, I would have sought medical discharge from the armed forces. Then I would have set my life direction on the path of studying psychology, especially criminology.

There is a 15 year old standing in front of you. What life advice would you give him/her?

You may listen to other people's opinions and advice, but only do what you think is right for yourself. We all make mistakes and that is how we learn to correct ourselves. Always be honest with yourself and others. Stay positive, reject negativity, and live life to the full. Be respectful and have love in your heart.

When you are an elderly person, sitting in your rocking chair and you look back on your life, what do you want to have achieved?

I would like to think that those who knew me still spoke about me.

Give me one word that sums up your life journey thus far: Content

What is the meaning of life?

To try and make a positive impact on the world and at the same time enjoy the journey. Other than that, 42.

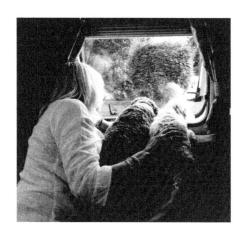

Name: Chandon 59
Age: 59 years
Gender: Female
Country: UK
Occupation: Retired

Do you believe in God?
No.

What is the worst thing you've ever done?
Got married the 1st time to a complete idiot (putting it mildly).

What is your greatest achievement?
Living & having my own business in Cyprus.

Tell me a secret about you:
I once had an affair with a married man.

If you could go back in time to age 20 with your current life experience, what would you do differently?

Emigrate to Australia.

There is a 15 year old standing in front of you. What life advice would you give him/her?

Do not ever smoke or take drugs.

When you are an elderly person, sitting in your rocking chair and you look back on your life, what do you want to have achieved?

To have had a good happy, fulfilling life with the one that I love.

Give me one word that sums up your life journey thus far: Experience

What is the meaning of life?

To find happiness.

Name: Clark

Age: 62

Gender: Male

Country: Ireland

Occupation: Editor

Do you believe in God?

No, because if God existed, she'd have better adverts. When I feel the need to exercise faith, I apply it to humanity.

What is the worst thing you've ever done?

When she needed me to be there for her in the lead-up to Uni, I let my daughter down in a major way. I was too far up my own arse to understand she was tugging at my sleeve.

What is your greatest achievement?

Even given the above failure, I worked hard at co-parenting two brilliant kids who frequently acknowledge their parents contribution to their success in life.

Tell me a secret about you:

My entire life I've often struggled to find reasons to do what others expect of me. Example: On my very first day of primary school, I got tired of waiting for the school doors to open that morning and walked off toward home.

If you could go back in time to age 20 with your current life experience, what would you do differently?

Not much. I'm very happy enjoying something very close to the meaning of life now, and wouldn't do anything to alter my course to the here and now.

There is a 15 year old standing in front of you. What life advice would you give him/her?

Always be clear in your head what you want to achieve, no matter how often those goals shift.

When you are an elderly person, sitting in your rocking chair and you look back on your life, what do you want to have achieved?

My kids once strongly advised me to achieve happiness. I'm near enough to that rocker to figure they predicted what I'll want to have achieved.

Give me one word that sums up your life journey thus far: Effort

What is the meaning of life?

Making sure those who love you know they're loved by you.

I'm fortunate to have recognised when I'd benefit from change in my life, and to have found the courage and means to go for it at those times. Honestly, those were all good choices.

It's equally important to also recognise that the proper change has been achieved, and how to then make the best of life.

Name: Sue D'Nimm

Age: My outlook: 33 -My physical: 73 My actual:53

Gender: Female

Country: South Africa for the first 33 years - England for the last 20 years

Occupation: Retired Healthcare Professional

Wife, mother, daughter, sister – not necessarily in that order. World traveller, textile crafter, day dreamer

Do you believe in God?

I believe there is a higher spirit, being, power. I believe that various religions have their gods, deities and divinities. I believe that people call their god by different names – Allah, Krishna, Om, Jehovah, Yahweh. I was brought up to believe in, and to call mine, God.

What is the worst thing you've ever done?

I broke someone's heart. Not like in a teenage kid kind of way, when you think the world is going to end and you will never find another love as great, and you lose your appetite, and you spend days listening to soppy ballads about lost or unrequited 'lurve', and spend hours looking at old photographs, and driving your friends around the bend with reminisces of the 'good' times while conveniently forgetting the bad times, and staring longingly across the school yard hoping he'll notice that you're looking fabulous because you're wearing mascara and 'juicy fruit' lip gloss (which are strictly not allowed), and wishing he would realise what he's missing and come grovelling back, but he's looking elsewhere, and you lock eyes with his friend, and all of a sudden the sun is shining just a bit brighter, and your appetite returns, and the photographs haven't been pulled out in a while, and the songs are all about falling in love, and the whole scenario begins again. Not like that at all. But in a life-changing, outlook-altering, earth-shattering way where literally the heart could be heard splintering into minuscule shards that can never be fully repaired because the cracks will always show, and some of the shards have permanently been misplaced but the heart still works to keep the body performing in a perfunctory manner, so to the outside world it seems intact, although from the inner circle the damage is so obvious that it seems like a miracle that it can even find the energy to beat, all the while knowing with every beat the pain is so excruciating that the heart would rather just stop and feel nothing. Ever. In that devastating way, when the sparkle behind the eyes turns to dust and there is a dullness that stares back in disbelief, where the smile will never again reach and the laughter lines become wrinkles of despair. When the world tilts on its axis and the Andreas fault lines give a huge shrug and the earth gives way beneath the feet and the spring in the step is forever lost, replaced instead with a measured tread mindful of each footfall, and each step placed with studious care and careful consideration never again to race along with carefree abandon or march joyously to the sound of their own drum. In that windpipe-crushing way, when all the air leaves the lungs and every breath is an epic asthma-like battle making the sound of a death-rattle because something has actually died inside but the pulmonary organs haven't got the message and valiantly keep trying to breathe, and that only sound made after the heart shattered is the rasping and gasping in a desperate attempt to get back on an even keel, but that can't happen because the once broad Atlas-esque shoulders that proudly carried countless hopes, dreams and expectations have sagged and bent under the weight of the worry and anxiety at the unexpected obliteration of future plans and ambitions, and the stoop is made more pronounced because the solar plexus has exploded as if punched by Mike Tyson and the 'fright or flight' instinct is so conflicted because the 'fright' just wants to scream and yell and curl up and die and the 'flight' wants to turn tail and run and run and run and never stop running. And all this annihilation happens in a split second, one instant, in that one moment of realisation. But the disintegration happens over time, falling apart piece by little piece, molecule by molecule, like a bottle of cola with a hole in the bottom trickling the contents away slowly, so slowly that the world barely notices until all that is left is the bottle, an empty bottle devoid of the fizz that once made it full of nothing but itself to offer. And all that is left is the emptiness and a shadow of the former self. And to witness this devastation as it folds is, in itself, a slow and painful process and the realisation where the responsibility lies is life-changing, outlook-altering and earth-shattering. I broke someone's heart and, by doing so, broke my own.

What is your greatest achievement?

This is where I should say 'my children', but they are not my greatest achievement, they are my proudest achievement.

My greatest achievement so far is that I've survived.

I survived horrendous bullying at school, that led to a half-baked attempt at a half-arsed attempt at suicide (which I survived).

I survived the awful diagnosis that my son was born with 'half a brain' (which turned out not to be true, although he does have a very complex genetic condition including the underdevelopment of his brain), and I survived his cranial surgery when he was 9 months old.

I survived the invasive battery of tests on my baby daughter including tests for cystic fibrosis and other life-limiting conditions,and surviving the culmination in surgery for oesophageal reconstruction when she was also only 9 months old.

I survived being held up at gunpoint and stabbed then drugged and locked up in the strong room while at work in a school.

I survived immigrating 6000 miles with 2 small children to country where I had no friends or family of my own, in the same week my beloved grandmother was buried.

I survived finding my closest friend dead on her bathroom floor when she was only 40 years young.

So, with a bit of help from prescription medication and the odd glass of whisky, in the words of Gloria Gaynor, 'I've got all my life to live, and all my love to give, I will survive'.

Tell me a secret about you:

No – secrets are not for telling.

If you could go back in time to age 20 with your current life experience, what would you do differently?

I would have pursued an entirely different career. Some people are lucky enough to know and follow their vocation from school leaving while others plod day to day never knowing the satisfaction of passionately enjoying their jobs. I count myself blessed to have found my ideal career but saddened that I was 40 by the time that happened. I only enjoyed my career for a short 10 years before having to retire due to ill health. I regret the 22 years I spent in jobs I didn't like, for people I didn't respect, in companies that didn't deserve me, for little or no job satisfaction.

There is a 15 year old standing in front of you. What life advice would you give him/her?

You are special, and unique. Your opinion matters. Don't let anyone put you down. Trust your instinct – if it feels wrong, it's wrong. Fulfil your potential to the best of your ability, otherwise you will eventually feel dissatisfied and discontent. Say sorry while you have the chance. Look after your health. Be kind. Do no harm.

When you are an elderly person, sitting in your rocking chair and you look back on your life, what do you want to have achieved?

There's not much more I'd like to achieve than I have already. I have brought my children up to adulthood and they are loving, good, solid people and decent members of society. I have a happy and stable marriage. I have wonderful relationships with my family and an amazing circle of friends. I've traveled far more than I ever imagined as a schoolgirl from Benoni, and intend to travel as much and for as long as possible. We are planning a quiet and relaxing retirement in warmer climes. So when I'm elderly in my rocking chair, I hope to be sitting with a smile on my face, with a glass of whisky in hand, eavesdropping on conversations and thinking 'Been there, done that!'

Give me one word that sums up your life journey thus far:

Rollercoaster. It's had ups and downs, but overall it's been a helluva ride!

What is the meaning of life?

Philosophers and sages, far wiser and more erudite than I am, have pondered this question through the ages. As far as I'm aware there is no one concise, unilateral answer. The question I prefer is, 'what is the purpose of life?' This has also been debated, but my personal opinion is that this is the question we as the human race should ask ourselves, not every day in prayer or every week in church, or even every once in a while among friends. It should become part of the fabric of life and, while I don't pretend to know all the questions or answers, should encompass at least the following:

Leave the world a bit better than you found it, by exploring your full potential and using it to leave behind something beautiful, whether it's a poem, a painting, recycling litter, or a daisy chain in a young girls hair. We all have the ability to leave something good and beautiful behind.

Do no harm.

Be kind.

And by doing these things, perhaps therein lies true happiness. What greater purpose is there than the pursuit of non-selfish, honestly philanthropic and, thereby, true happiness?

Name: Orlaff of Moose or DA to those that know me.

Age: 57

Gender: I could do with a little help on both age and gender- one a lot more so than the other.

Country: United Kingdom

Occupation: Art Director/Photographer/Writer/Musician/ Sage

Do you believe in God?

Can't be certain about this one either way; yet to be convinced.

What is the worst thing you've ever done?

It's not necessarily the worst thing: When I was seven, I had a good friend at school. We were waiting with our bikes to cross an unmanned pedestrian crossing over a railway line. We asked a lady if it was all clear to go, she said there was a train coming. We waited for it to pass and started to cross. My friend went first, a train hit him coming in the opposite direction. There was nothing anyone could do. I should've looked, and known to look. It just never occurred. If I'd seen, I could have perhaps shouted or done something. I have always felt guilty and have deep regret for that life lost. It could so easily been me that crossed the line first.Not a long time after; a footbridge was put in. No-one has been killed at that point since.

This I am ashamed of, sad about and regret.

What is your greatest achievement?

My two children and my part in the people they are.

Tell me a secret about you:

I have a very large pet Monstera Deliciosa (Giant Swiss Cheese) plant named Gerald who is now a lot older and somewhat better looking than quite a number of people I know.

If you could go back in time to age 20 with your current life experience, what would you do differently?

The bad stuff; Virtually Everything

The good stuff: Virtually Nothing

What about my teens? Some of it was brilliant and rather dodgy.

There is a 15 year old standing in front of you. What life advice would you give him/her?

Find yourself and your space in the world; but there's no rush, it will happen.

When you are an elderly person, sitting in your rocking chair and you look back on your life, what do you want to have achieved?

To be known as a good man.

Give me one word that sums up your life journey thus far: Uniqueness

What is the meaning of life?

43. Douglas Adams was only one out, so close; but he did once state:

"This is an interesting world I find myself in—an interesting hole I find myself in—fits me rather neatly, doesn't it? In fact it fits me staggeringly well, must have been made to have me in it!"

DA once thought: "Happiness and loving whenever it is possible."

Name: Debbie Clarke

Age: 38

Gender: Female

Country: UK

Occupation: Business coach

Do you believe in God?

Nope.

What is the worst thing you've ever done?

Shouting at my daughter in a rage is by far the worst thing I've ever done. It embarrasses me and makes me feel ashamed when I think about it.

What is your greatest achievement?

My daughter Robin, she's amazing, feisty, independent and loving.

Tell me a secret about you:

I like going to bed early.

If you could go back in time to age 20 with your current life experience, what would you do differently?

I wouldn't do anything differently, because if I had I wouldn't be the same person. You change one tiny thing and the whole thing would unravel and start to change. You have to learn to live with what you've got, that's when you start to feel comfortable with yourself.

There is a 15 year old standing in front of you. What life advice would you give him/her?

It's all going to be ok. Just ride it out lovely, I'm here waiting for you x

When you are an elderly person, sitting in your rocking chair and you look back on your life, what do you want to have achieved?

Calm and peace of mind.

Give me one word that sums up your life journey thus far: Effervescent

What is the meaning of life?

There is no meaning, you make your own meaning.

Just enjoy it, be nice to people, be kind to yourself.

Name: Dave
Age: 61
Gender: Male
Country: England
Occupation: DJ

Do you believe in God?
Yes.

What is the worst thing you've ever done?
Gone in a casino.

What is your greatest achievement?

Won you back offa Jeremy, back in the day.

Tell me a secret about you:

Really grieving behind the smile.

If you could go back in time to age 20 with your current life experience, what would you do differently?

I would hit London.

There is a 15 year old standing in front of you. What life advice would you give him/her?

Live and cherish every day.

When you are an elderly person, sitting in your rocking chair and you look back on your life, what do you want to have achieved?

Happiness to a degree.

Give me one word that sums up your life journey thus far: Confused

What is the meaning of life?

To maintain the species.

Just like to add..... that it takes ages for the penny to drop...

Anyway, too late now.

Name: Grounded Carer

Age: 55

Gender: Female

Country: UK

Occupation: Financial advisor / mortgage arranger

Do you believe in God?

Well it depends how you define God. If you're asking me if there's a man that sits on a cloud and looks after us then the answer is no but if God is the meaning of good, then yes.

What is the worst thing you've ever done?

The worst thing I think I ever did was nick some money from my Dads money pot. With that money I took a taxi to

Leicester to visit my PE teacher who was off school sick – I adored her. I had no idea how I was gonna get home as I spent all the money on the taxi there. Thankfully, she took me home after her boyfriend turned up (which really upset me) Turns out the money wasn't my Dad's it was the fishing clubs and my Dad had to refund it. I never owned up. Until now.

What is your greatest achievement?

I'm not going to say work but I would say my sporting achievements: Playing hockey for the region and captaining the side.

Tell me a secret about you:

When I was with a woman, she went away on a course and I couldn't get hold of her and I knew she was up to no good. It turned out she was messing about with this bloke who was a director of a recruitment company. She was looking for another job, via him, so I rang him up the following week and pretended to be her saying I didn't want to continue looking for a job anymore so he'd leave her alone. Don't know if he did because we split up shortly after.

If you could go back in time to age 20 with your current life experience, what would you do differently?

I wouldn't cheat. I'd have got more qualifications: less time on the sports field and more time in the classroom. Travelled more.

There is a 15 year old standing in front of you. What life advice would you give him/her?

Be caring about others and kind. Go as far as you can. Listen to advice. Always strive to do better.

When you are an elderly person, sitting in your rocking chair and you look back on your life, what do you want to have achieved?

Now this is where I'm not very good. My life as I see it is to try and be happy and try and make other people happy. As long as I've done that I think I've achieved.

Give me one word that sums up your life journey thus far: Caring

What is the meaning of life?

Fuck knows! I don't know that there is a meaning of life. Just do the best that you can. If your expectations are too high you just get sad.

I think there's two types of people: There's people that are always searching, looking for answers – thinkers. Over thinkers that rip the arse out of everything, and then there's the rest of us who keep the thinkers on a grounded level.

Name: David Macaulay

Age: 50

Gender: Male

Country: United States

Occupation: Writer and marketer

Do you believe in God?

Not in the Christian sense.

What is the worst thing you've ever done?

Put kippers in the bed of my college roommate who suffered from a fish allergy.

What is your greatest achievement?

Ensuring my kids are model citizens most days of the week.

Tell me a secret about you:

I spent most of my fifth year wearing a bucket on my head. It seemed cool at the time.

If you could go back in time to age 20 with your current life experience, what would you do differently?

I would have avoided marriage until I was at least 50-years-old

There is a 15 year old standing in front of you. What life advice would you give him/her?

Take a year off to see the world. Then focus on a career that won't be replaced by robots.

When you are an elderly person, sitting in your rocking chair and you look back on your life, what do you want to have achieved?

I'd like my one or two great unfinished novels to be staring back at me from the book shelf in finished form.

Give me one word that sums up your life journey thus far: Haphazard

What is the meaning of life?

Take a step back, smell the roses or hydrangeas, and don't take yourself too seriously. Very few people will care to remember you six months after you are gone anyway.

Name: Denise

Age: 59

Gender: Female

Country: England

Occupation: Shop owner

Do you believe in God?

Sometimes... as in when 'God' took my husband at the age of 55 and then my mother 2 months later.... why did he create so much hurt?

What is the worst thing you've ever done?

Slept with a friends boyfriend.

What is your greatest achievement?

My twin daughters. I became infertile at the age of 30 having had 2 ectopic pregnancies - one that was life threatening. 5 x IVF treatments. Five days before my 40th birthday I gave birth to my twin girls.

Tell me a secret about you:

I can read people and see their auras.

If you could go back in time to age 20 with your current life experience, what would you do differently?

Learn how to say "no".

There is a 15 year old standing in front of you. What life advice would you give him/her?

Learn how to say "no" again.

When you are an elderly person, sitting in your rocking chair and you look back on your life, what do you want to have achieved?

To bring my family back together again.

Give me one word that sums up your life journey thus far: Struggling

What is the meaning of life?

To give life a meaning.

Glenn was my first boyfriend when I was 17. We got engaged when I was 18. He left me for a woman who he met whilst in the army, she got pregnant and he married her. 27 years later he came back into my life. Two years later we married. 4 years later he passed away. I regret none of it as I wouldn't be standing here now, having had a great career in TV, twins of 19 from a previous marriage and an OK- ish life.

Name: Dean

Age: 54

Gender: Male

Country: The country of the imagination or the USA

Occupation: US Federal Government apparatchik.

Do you believe in God?

NO. IMO, God is a human construct designed to fill the space in our mind occupied by doubt, fear and the incomprehensible. I would sooner believe in a responsible agent. At least it's manifestly obvious that man did not create life, much less the universe.

What is the worst thing you've ever done?

Walked past a car accident without rendering aid.

What is your greatest achievement?

Aided in the identification and repatriation of 230 dead Marines killed by a terrorist bombing in Beirut.

Tell me a secret about you:

My soulmate is gone. I will love her for the rest of my life.

If you could go back in time to age 20 with your current life experience, what would you do differently?

To be of value and benefit to those less endowed with the knowledge of life's mysteries. Lift up those who fall. Lead by example. Expand the bubble of love.

There is a 15 year old standing in front of you. What life advice would you give him/her?

Incorporate the wisdom of those who have traveled life's journey before you; never surrender the chance to experience your own journey; enrich the experience of those who come after you.

When you are an elderly person, sitting in your rocking chair and you look back on your life, what do you want to have achieved?

To have meaningfully and lastingly enriched the existence of contemporaries and those souls yet to experience the breath of future life.

Give me one word that sums up your life journey thus far: Providential

What is the meaning of life?

Life is a blank canvas. It was not created by God but by random circumstance. Your life is your masterpiece or it's a portrait of your Dorian Gray. It will hang in the hall of honor where it will please and puzzle future souls. Or... it will be trodden into dust by the feet of countless billions, and be forever after as completely unknown as the name of the first soul to stare upon a star.

If God is a myth perpetrated by the fear of the unknown, if faith can only be a vehicle of the self, if the meaning of life can only be determined by human intent and thus divined by the intellect, how will you resolve the panorama of what your life can be?

Name: Dancing Queen

Age: 72

Gender: Female

Country: UK

Occupation: Retired

Do you believe in God?

When my father died I could not believe that He could let that happen, but as time went on I felt it quite easy to talk to my Dad through God and found this helped me a lot. I still talk to my Dad on most days even if it is to say good morning or good night.

What is the worst thing you've ever done?

When my I heard my Dad was in hospital I was called by the police to see him as a matter of urgency. I didn't want anyone to come with me so I travelled up to where he lived but arrived quite late. I had to decide if I should go to see my Dad or go straight to see my Mum. At the time I thought my Mum needed me as my Dad was in safe hands in hospital, he died that night.

What is your greatest achievement?

Getting married to my husband, it was the happiest day of my life, but dancing with the Royal Ballet at Stratford upon Avon when I was at college was very special to me and I felt proud to be chosen.

Tell me a secret about you:

When my Mum died I found out that I was born out of wedlock. My Father was still my Dad but they were not married as my Father was waiting for his divorce to come through. At the time I was very shocked.

If you could go back in time to age 20 with your current life experience, what would you do differently?

My only wish was that I'd have known that I couldn't have children.

There is a 15 year old standing in front of you. What life advice would you give him/her?

To work hard, enjoy life, be respectful to others, this is not a rehearsal.

When you are an elderly person, sitting in your rocking chair and you look back on your life, what do you want to have achieved?

I am! To have enjoyed my life and to bring as much happiness as I can to other people.

Give me one word that sums up your life journey thus far: Wonderful

What is the meaning of life?

Everyone is put in this world for a purpose and I feel that everyone should try to be good to each other- but life isn't like that. I also think that when you die it is God's way of telling you that you have achieved your duties of life on earth.

Name: Duncan Bradford

Age: 47

Gender: Male

Country: United Kingdom

Occupation: Serial Entrepreneur / Managing Director

Do you believe in God?

Absolutely not.

What is the worst thing you've ever done?

Firstly, I want to apologise that most of my answers will be business related. I'm not obsessed with making money by any means, but business has been such a large part of my life to date that it's bound to show in my answers.

The worst thing I have ever done is start an estate agency business 3 years before the 2008 recession and as a result nearly went bankrupt.

What is your greatest achievement?

Besides the obvious answer any parent would/should say, had to wonderful children, my greatest achievement must be planning, building and launching Ukandoo Academy, which has been a life long dream. It shows that keeping sight of your dreams and vision no matter what hardships you face along the way, will result in you achieving them one day.

Tell me a secret about you:

Wow a hard one. I LOVE musicals! I've been shot at 3 times, hit once. Other than my children, my greatest love is for the environment.

If you could go back in time to age 20 with your current life experience, what would you do differently?

I wouldn't waste my time & money at university like I did. I would be braver in business as at that age you have nothing to lose. I would focus on a location independent business and lifestyle from the very start rather than having premises and fixed overheads. I wouldn't waste my time and energy doing things I don't enjoy.

There is a 15 year old standing in front of you. What life advice would you give him/her?

Don't listen to what school, friends, family, and society tells you to do with YOUR life because that's what 'SHOULD' be done. Instead, follow your heart, dreams, and own path. Make your own story and most importantly, ensure you enjoy what you do. Life is about building memorable experiences, doing good things, helping to make the world a better place, not about just working like a slave doing something you don't enjoy.

When you are an elderly person, sitting in your rocking chair and you look back on your life, what do you want to have achieved?

I want to have achieved financial freedom, and not be reliant on anyone, or the state, for money during my retirement. Financial freedom doesn't have a number attached to it. It's not about being a millionaire or having any kind of pompous status. It's simply about having the means to live without work or support in a lifestyle of your choosing, which for me is fairly simple as I'm not materialistic.

I would also like to have a lasting business legacy for which I feel proud to have created and that genuinely helps society in some way.

I would want to have done my part in helping to improve the world and natural habitats through donations, conservation work, environment protection, and any other ways I could contribute throughout my life. I am 47 years old now and I have donated to wildlife and conservation projects every month since I was 18 years old, without a break, no matter how close to bankruptcy I got a couple of times. For me this is extremely important and my donations one of my first expense priorities.

And finally I would want to have had happy and healthy children who grow up to be inspirational to others.

Give me one word that sums up your life journey thus far: Challenging / Rollercoaster

What is the meaning of life?

The meaning of life for me is 3 part; enjoying life, achieving your dreams, and making a positive impact on the world.

Name: Soul Girl

Age: 48

Gender: Female

Country: UK

Occupation: Nurse

Do you believe in God?

No because I've seen too much misery heaped on great people & too much fortune given to arseholes. If there is a God it isn't the God that religion tells of, who loves us all. This God is a sick sadist who plays with lives for fun, it seems.

What is the worst thing you've ever done?

The thing I'm most ashamed of is betraying the trust of those who have trusted me.

What is your greatest achievement?

Having the determination to become a nurse as a 'mature' student. I had to give up full time employment & return to college for a year, then move from my home town to train for 3 years.

Tell me a secret about you:

I have a bodywarmer…

If you could go back in time to age 20 with your current life experience, what would you do differently?

Make different decisions regarding my relationships and not stay in an unfulfilling relationship for fear of being on my own.

There is a 15 year old standing in front of you. What life advice would you give him/her?

It would depend if the 15 year old asked for my advice!

But I would say always believe in yourself but don't take yourself too seriously & don't let anyone put you down - especially teachers.

When you are an elderly person, sitting in your rocking chair and you look back on your life, what do you want to have achieved?

If I become elderly that in itself will be an achievement as my lifestyle isn't exactly conducive to a long life! However if I do make it, I will be happy if I keep all my faculties, remain continent & laugh out loud every single day.

Give me one word that sums up your life journey thus far: Lucky

What is the meaning of life?

I don't think there is one. I think life is a random series of events that are overanalysed to give some meaning to our mundane existence.

Life is about laughter. When I told my best friend I owned a body warmer she put down her drink and left the pub. I thought we'd never speak again. An item of clothing without sleeves is utterly pointless, she said. We had agreed on this for years but I secretly bought one. I said I'd burn it but then we decided we would start up the "Global Body Warmer Challenge" instead and send it around the world to be put on as many interesting things as possible.

Name: Fred
Age: 51
Gender: Male
Country: England (Spain now)
Occupation: Business Teacher (in English)

Do you believe in God?
No - and pity those that do.

What is the worst thing you've ever done?
Stolen my father's car.

What is your greatest achievement?
Leaving the railway and emigrating to Spain. Otherwise, passing my teaching certificate first time.

Tell me a secret about you:

I lent a friend £2000 which she paid back over two years. She didn't even thank me.

If you could go back in time to age 20 with your current life experience, what would you do differently?

Buy a house with no garden - easy maintenance - then buy another.

There is a 15 year old standing in front of you. What life advice would you give him/her?

Learn another language. Or two. Don't grow up too fast either.

When you are an elderly person, sitting in your rocking chair and you look back on your life, what do you want to have achieved?

Respect from my students (who, on the whole, love me).

Give me one word that sums up your life journey thus far: Diverse

What is the meaning of life?

Love, financial security and quality rumpy-pumpy.

Name: Jacki

Age: 55

Gender: Female

Country: USA

Occupation: Writer of Poetry and Children's Stories.

Do you believe in God?

Yes. I believe in Jesus, actually & to me, there is a difference. In my mind, "God" has always seemed something to be feared. Maybe because I was raised Catholic ? Maybe not …"Jesus" though, is truly my friend and has been for a very long while. I also believe in reincarnation. I feel I have and will continue to live many, many lives with my end result, eventually, being "Jesus" "Heaven" or whatever name we would like to call it.

What is the worst thing you've ever done?

I don't really have too many regrets because I believe everything really does happen for a reason. I feel I am exactly where I am supposed to be at this moment, warts and all. Having said that though, I often wish I would have picked up an acoustic guitar years ago. I'm teaching myself how to play one now. The feeling I feel when I strum my guitar makes me wish I'd have listened to my guitar playing inner voice a long time ago.

What is your greatest achievement?

My children and my writing.

Tell me a secret about you:

I'm terribly introverted.

If you could go back in time to age 20 with your current life experience, what would you do differently?

Live somewhere in or around the Rocky Mountains. Had I seen that beauty when I was 20 years old, I never would have left.

There is a 15 year old standing in front of you. What life advice would you give him/her?

To absolutely listen to your inner voice. Follow your heart wherever it takes you & don't worry about what anyone else thinks.

When you are an elderly person, sitting in your rocking chair and you look back on your life, what do you want to have achieved?

I hope to leave my mark on the world with my poetry and children's stories.

Give me one word that sums up your life journey thus far: Zig- zaggy.

What is the meaning of life?

To find, treasure and stay in tune with your inner self. It makes for a happier life.

This isn't important or relevant to your book but, I want you to know I enjoyed answering your questions. Thanks for asking!

Name: An Englishman in California

Age: 48

Gender: Male

Country: USA

Occupation: Self-employed general Contractor … yep I build other people's shit!!!

Do you believe in God?

I don't believe in God the same way main stream believes God. To think there is one almighty God does not ring true to me. If God was another word for energy I can get my head around that as everything is made up of energy, It's all around us. So that's why I don't go to the house of God every Sunday and listen to yet another interpretation of what was written 2000+ years ago. So, I see God as concept of universal spiritual energy similar to the native Americans.

What is the worst thing you've ever done?

This is a trick question as I can always incriminate myself with something out of the corner of my darkest closet or talk about the body recoveries I've done over the years volunteering my services with search and rescue. Ok, so it's not incriminating but it's not something I'm proud of. When I was in Desert Storm (as a royal engineer in the British army) after the big 'shock and aww' we had pushed Sadam's army out of Kuwait. Our section was given the assignment of clearing a base camp of booby traps and IED's for the British liaison team to come and do their thing. This we did in a very efficient way, but one problem was it was overrun with feral cats (nasty disease, flea ridden cats). We could not shoot them as we had to account for every round so we used a flare gun. I'll never forget the smell of burning fur and sadistic meows as the cats arched through the air in a rainbow of phosphorus sparks. Like I said, it is not something I am proud of, but we were putting the poor things out of their misery.

What is your greatest achievement?

Raising my kids thus far. They survived all the adventures of growing up without being too traumatize by a dad that liked to live on the edge!They have calmed my passion for excitement and given me so much more than just responsibility.

My 22-year-old daughter Makena (named after Makena Cove in Maui where I married my wife on the beach) has taught me patience and understanding and the meaning of being unselfish. She is an amazing artist and fashion designer. My son Avery (named after Avery Ranch where

I proposed to my wife) has such passion for life and having fun. We spend many days together training with SAR, snowboarding or fishing, He's off to University of Idaho.

Tell me a secret about you:

I had sex with a horse once. Just kidding, the damn thing kept running away!

If I told you a secret about me, it would no longer be a secret however … Love having sex outdoors! Oh, yerr baby!

If you could go back in time to age 20 with your current life experience, what would you do differently?

Have more sex outdoors! Take a year off and travel the world before having kids and then I would buy real estate … fix and hold …. fix and flip and play a real-life game of Monopoly.

There is a 15-year-old standing in front of you. What life advice would you give him/her?

Boy: Put a condom on your pecker until you want babies.

Girl: Put a condom on his pecker until you want to have babies.

Read Rich Dad Poor Dad.

Don't get brainwashed into thinking you go to school, go to college, get a good job and climb the corporate ladder. JOB stands for Just over broke by the way. Think outside the box and love what you do and do what you love. The universal law of attraction will give you everything you need. Most important is HAVE FUN! Do all this and you will earn an M.B.A. (Massive Bank Account)

When you are an elderly person, sitting in your rocking chair and you look back on your life, what do you want to have achieved?

We are only physically on this planet for such a small amount of time in the general scope of things so by the time I can no longer run, walk, crawl or drive a scooter, I want to have seen, eaten, touched, heard as many different experiences as possible.

Give me one word that sums up your life journey thus far: Bloody Brilliant -Oops that's 2, sorry!

What is the meaning of life?

I must laugh because the first thing that comes to mind is Monty Python's "Always look on the bright side of life"

To me, the meaning of life is true love in any shape, fashion or form.

Name: Jaine Chappel

Age: 56

Gender: Female

Country: United Kingdom

Occupation: Social Worker

Do you believe in God?

No.

What is the worst thing you've ever done?

Put my mum into a home.

What is your greatest achievement?

Having my amazing son, Jake.

Tell me a secret about you:

I keep secrets so can't tell.

If you could go back in time to age 20 with your current life experience, what would you do differently?

I would buy property (in Sheffield and ,London)

I would go to college and uni (earlier than I did)

I would start a profession at that age rather than wait until older.

I would go to festivals at an earlier age (as I've loved the ones I've been to but didn't go to one until older)

I would travel from an earlier age.

I would appreciate my mum more.

I would have more children.

There is a 15 year old standing in front of you. What life advice would you give him/her?

Get a career earlier in life

Enjoy yourself and have fun/don't take life too seriously.

Travel.

Make good friends.

Spend as much time as you can with your family.

When you are an elderly person, sitting in your rocking chair and you look back on your life, what do you want to have achieved?

To have seen many countries and enjoyed life.

Give me one word that sums up your life journey thus far: Changeable

What is the meaning of life?

Fuck knows.

You will never be happy if you continue to search for what happiness consists of. You will never live if you are looking for the meaning of life.

Name: Jase

Age: 51

Gender: Alpha male

Country: UK

Occupation: Truck driver

Do you believe in God?

Yes.

What is the worst thing you've ever done?

Beating someone half to death in my younger years.

What is your greatest achievement?

Being a dad.

Tell me a secret about you:

I was abused as a child.

If you could go back in time to age 20 with your current life experience, what would you do differently?

Nothing. Every experience has made me the person I am.

There is a 15 year old standing in front of you. What life advice would you give him/her?

Do things in life that make you happy, be it work or love.

When you are an elderly person, sitting in your rocking chair and you look back on your life, what do you want to have achieved?

Living long enough to see my own kids marry and have their own family.

Give me one word that sums up your life journey thus far: Difficult

What is the meaning of life?

From being born the clock is ticking to when you die. Fill that time with passion and love. Very few of us know when our final day will be.

Name: Jane

Age: 53

Gender: Female

Country: England

Occupation: Clinical support worker

Do you believe in God?

I believe there is something, I am a spiritual person so I believe in energy. There is something that no one can explain but I am an open minded person.

What is the worst thing you've ever done?

To be completely honest I have done things when I was younger and maybe not in a good situation that I am not very proud of, but to name one thing, I don't think I can. I do believe that we all learn from the things we do, whether it be wrong or right, and it makes us grow as a person.

What is your greatest achievement?

My children.

Tell me a secret about you:

I'm still learning to love my self !!

If you could go back in time to age 20 with your current life experience, what would you do differently?

Maybe a few things but the choices I have made and the roads I have gone down were the ones I needed to learn my life's journey and know what I know to become the woman I am today.

There is a 15 year old standing in front of you. What life advice would you give him/her?

To love her self is I feel one of the most important things, helps to be confidant and independent. To be kind to people and animals.

When you are an elderly person, sitting in your rocking chair and you look back on your life, what do you want to have achieved?

To have seen my children happy and living fulfilled lives whatever they choose to do. To have found the love of my life and to have been loved.

Give me one word that sums up your life journey thus far: "work in progress" sorry that's 3 words but couldn't think of one.

What is the meaning of life?

To love and be loved.

Thank you for asking me to do this Jules, it has really made me think of life and where I am going and where I want to be. There are so many things going on in our lives that we often forget to just be.

Name: Jed Southgate

Age: 60

Gender: Male

Country: England

Occupation: Man of Mystery

Do you believe in God?

No.

What is the worst thing you've ever done?

Trust a liar (business partner)

What is your greatest achievement?

Having three kids who still talk to me.

Tell me a secret about you:

I'm not a virgin.

If you could go back in time to age 20 with your current life experience, what would you do differently?

Not work so much.

There is a 15 year old standing in front of you. What life advice would you give him/her?

Look forward always, never look back.

When you are an elderly person, sitting in your rocking chair and you look back on your life, what do you want to have achieved?

The ability not to soil myself.

Give me one word that sums up your life journey thus far: Fab

What is the meaning of life?

42

Name: Jane Satterwhite

Age: 56

Gender: Female

Country: USA

Occupation: Medical

Do you believe in God?

Yes, I will be the first to say it has been tough especially this past year when my grandson Jaxon passed away when he was 6 weeks old. I couldn't understand how my loving God could cause so much hurt to my children and our whole family in this devastation. I know in my heart there is a reason not sure I will ever understand but I know God has been there every step of the way helping me work thru this. I realize the walls I built up were not God's doing it was the Devil trying to keep me from God's love and healing hands.

What is the worst thing you've ever done?

This is a hard question there are many things that I have done wrong in my life but I have always had God's never ending love and forgiveness for the things I have done. I've been divorced, lied to my parents, failed in my college with no reason but wanting to be a rebel in my own world.

What is your greatest achievement?

My children, I love my 3 girls they have taught me life's ups and downs and the greatest rewards watching them grow and become who they are.

Tell me a secret about you:

I don't have any real secrets, I am a rather open book. Maybe the hurt I have had in the past 2 years with losing my brother, then grandson last year and a month ago, my Mom. I try to be strong during these times but there are days I struggle to keep the smile and keep going. I miss them all so much. I also miss my Dad he has been gone since 1996 and there are days I just want to have a little conversation with him.

If you could go back in time to age 20 with your current life experience, what would you do differently?

I don't know that I would do anything a lot different. Maybe study harder and accomplish my career goals. But wouldn't change my girls for anything or my life's experiences.

There is a 15 year old standing in front of you. What life advice would you give him/her?

Never take life or loved ones for granted!! Tell them you love them because tomorrow is never promised. Go after your dreams you can achieve anything you want...but you have to work at it. Always love God...he is always forgiving and loving....LISTEN.

When you are an elderly person, sitting in your rocking chair and you look back on your life, what do you want to have achieved?

My children's respect and love, my grandchildren to know I love them with unending love. I have completed my life's journey with my life partner Charles, even though our lives took different roads at the beginning the fact that God brought us together and our families together has been nothing short of fabulous. We just enjoy being together and I have been able to witness his baptism into the Holy Spirit and his faith growing in leaps and bounds. We are so "Blessed" to have the Texas Cowboy Church as our church family.

Give me one word that sums up your life journey thus far: Wholesome

What is the meaning of life?

Life is what you make it....the trials, tribulations, and the road that you travel in your years here on earth. Your spirit and everlasting love of our Lord and his miracles that he teaches us each and everyday. Life is your day by day story to which you are the main character and author.

Name: Under construction.

Age: Old enough

Gender: Male

Country: USA

Occupation: Construction supervisor

Do you believe in God?

I do believe in God. This life, this world and this universe just seem too incredible to have been done without a Creator. I even pray on occasion. When people die, I hope they go to Heaven. The cynic in me thinks that God created all and then put it all away in the biggest of trunks. Occasionally, He pulls the universe out and turns a cold eye our way. Hating not, loving not, as Caliban said, just a hint of curiosity about how we've turned paradise into a polluted parking lot. The optimist hopes it's all amounts to something and slowly but surely climbing above the muck. One day rising above the brim to see it all as God sees it.

What is the worst thing you've ever done?

My greatest regret is spanking my son. I did it several times through his childhood. It didn't amount to beating, but corporal punishment, usually to stop a tantrum or complete obstinance. He was the child though and I the adult. I should've done better and if I could only take back one thing I did in my whole life (and there's a lengthy list of misdeeds and sins), this is what I would take back.

What is your greatest achievement?

Having said that, I think my children are my greatest achievement. I've spent a lifetime building skyscrapers in NYC, but I care not a thousandth for them as I do my kids. They're not quite adults yet, not fully developed, but they fill me with joy and pride.

Tell me a secret about you:

A secret: I once seriously considered suicide. It was the day after Thanksgiving a few years ago. I was standing on the roof of a building. I was alone up there and felt utterly desolate and crushed. It was the lowest point of my divorce and my wife was threatening to take my children from me. I was afraid she'd be successful. I don't consider myself to have suicidal tendencies or even to be depressed, but for that one day all of the good things seemed to have totally ebbed away, like the ocean before a tsunami. After standing up there by the parapet for a couple of hours, I knew I couldn't leave my children. Really, the thought that brought me back to my senses was the fact that the children of a suicide are at a much greater risk to succumbing themselves. So I chose to fight and never let myself think that way again.

If you could go back in time to age 20 with your current life experience, what would you do differently?

If I could go back to 20 year old me, I would take college far more seriously and see the Clash far more often.

There is a 15 year old standing in front of you. What life advice would you give him/her?

If I was talking to a 15-year-old (my daughter is 14 and my son is 20, so I do experience this), I'd say, "Be much kinder and more respectful to your family, especially your parents. They're much smarter than you think. And, no, you're not the first one to have that particular experience."

When you are an elderly person, sitting in your rocking chair and you look back on your life, what do you want to have achieved?

As an old man, I'd think it quite an achievement to have attained contentment sitting by a fire, reading a good book, and sipping a nice, hot tea. Also, I'd like to be satisfied I had left behind my children as two functioning and responsible adults.

Give me one word that sums up your life journey thus far: Procrastination

What is the meaning of life?

I don't know really. I'm feeling a bit pessimistic at the moment, so I might say there is no meaning, at least for the vast majority of us. If 99.999999999% of us had never lived, would the world be any better or worse off. The amount of people who cause even the slightest ripple beyond their own generation is infinitesimally small. The meaning of life is to be, so try to be at least happy while doing it. Blah!

Name: Janet

Age: 69

Gender: Female

Country: England

Occupation: Retired

Do you believe in God?

No I do not believe in God. I did when I was young but having been married for 47 years to an extreme anti theist I no longer believe in a god. However I do believe in altruism. I have a caring and nurturing nature. I worked for 25 years helping special needs children to cope with mainstream education and social issues.

What is the worst thing you've ever done?

The worst thing I have ever done is accidentally broken six bottles of my husband's home made wine. He was underneath his car at the time trying to do a major repair.

He was not amused!!!

What is your greatest achievement?

Giving birth ,nurturing loving and always being there for my two children who are now parents themselves.

Tell me a secret about you:

I would have married George Clooney if he had asked me !!!

If you could go back in time to age 20 with your current life experience, what would you do differently?

I would have travelled more and been open to new experiences such as parachute jumping!

There is a 15 year old standing in front of you. What life advice would you give him/her?

My advice would to believe in yourself and the choices you make. To take opportunities as they arise and enjoy every moment of the success that you achieve. Remember to have fun too.

When you are an elderly person, sitting in your rocking chair and you look back on your life, what do you want to have achieved?

I am an old person but still feel young and full of life.

When I was in my teens I wanted to fall in love, have a beautiful home. To have children and grandchildren all of which I have achieved. My sadness is that my parents both died aged 65 and never saw their grandchildren grow up.

Give me one word that sums up your life journey thus far: Contentment

What is the meaning of life?

I feel life is the opportunity to believe in yourself, to set your own goals, to love, to share, to care, to be happy and help other people to do the same.

Name: John

Age: 73

Gender: Male

Country: England

Occupation: Company director

Do you believe in God?

How can one believe in a deity that allows genocide, the holocaust, wars, abuse of adults and children, disease etc etc.

What is the worst thing you've ever done?

Poor relationship with my father.

What is your greatest achievement?

Helping to create many jobs.

Tell me a secret about you:

I hated school and frequently caused disruption and trouble but was constantly "bailed out" by my cousin who was School Captain.

If you could go back in time to age 20 with your current life experience, what would you do differently?

Read philosophy at university rather than pharmacology.

There is a 15 year old standing in front of you. What life advice would you give him/her?

Don't let others tell you what to do and be true to yourself but without being selfish or bad mannered.

When you are an elderly person, sitting in your rocking chair and you look back on your life, what do you want to have achieved?

To have lived a mannered life behaving with others as I would want to be treated.

Give me one word that sums up your life journey thus far: Frustrated

What is the meaning of life?

I have absolutely no idea but possibly 42!

Reiterate the mantra "do unto others………."

Name: Janet Lebeck Janovich

Age: 67

Gender: Female

Country: United States of America

Occupation: Retired Postal Worker

Do you believe in God?

I believe in God the Father, Jesus his son and The Holy Spirit

What is the worst thing you've ever done?

The worse thing I ever did in my life: Didn't tell my parents I was raped on my 16th Birthday.

What is your greatest achievement?

Motherhood. I became a mother at 17. They wanted me to give the baby up for adoption. Something I could not or would not do. I proved I was a provider for my children. Sometimes a single Mom but I was always there for them. Against all odds but we made it. The love I have for my children is never ending. My grandchildren and great grandchildren are proof that miracles continue.

Tell me a secret about you:

I have no home to go too. I am currently homeless spending time between my granddaughter's and daughters house.

If you could go back in time to age 20 with your current life experience, what would you do differently?

If I could go back 20 years I would have shaved my head for my daughter and never left he side.

There is a 15 year old standing in front of you. What life advice would you give him/her?

I married at 17 and thought my life would have a white picket fence and yellow roses. Wait until your older for a serious relationship. You have so much life to live.

When you are an elderly person, sitting in your rocking chair and you look back on your life, what do you want to have achieved?

I am elderly. I hope I have achieved being a good mother and Nana. Show my children that God and Jesus are the true way to Heaven. To love each other and be there for each other after I'm gone.

Give me one word that sums up your life journey thus far: Blessed

What is the meaning of life?

Life's meaning is watching new life after death. Knowing one day we will understand why things happened this way. Knowing there is a better life awaiting us.

I have held a dead grandchild in my arms and witnessed the grief in Sons eyes. I have seen the joy in those same eyes after his next child was born.

I have watched my own daughter die and wondered why God didn't take me instead. I have been blessed to be a great grandmother, a lot of people don't have that same privilege. I have loved and losses but one thing is true: Never in this journey did God forsake me or leave my side.

Name: John Kretlow

Age: 73

Gender: Male

Country: U.S

Occupation: Retired

Do you believe in God?

Yes, I can't believe this earth is just an accident. I believe God had something specific in mind.

What is the worst thing you've ever done?

I killed 13 men in Vietnam and, although I was just doing my job, I still feel regret at taking the lives of 13 human beings.

What is your greatest achievement?

On a purely secular basis, I graduated from University, made it through Vietnam, had two kids, and retired after 30 years of service in a large oil company. On a spiritual basis, I was fortunate enough to hear and believe the word of God, so I came out of the darkness into the light.

Tell me a secret about you:

I'm a chocoholic.

If you could go back in time to age 20 with your current life experience, what would you do differently?

I would have stayed away from alcohol and tobacco and led a more tranquil and moral life.

There is a 15 year old standing in front of you. What life advice would you give him/her?

I would tell her to avoid drugs and tobacco and drink only in moderation. I would urge her to get as much education as possible and get into a good bible believing church and get assurance of her salvation as Jesus is coming soon in the rapture. Also,I would warn her about pier pressure.

When you are an elderly person, sitting in your rocking chair and you look back on your life, what do you want to have achieved?

I would like to have made a difference in someone's life. I would like to feel that someone's life has been better because of having been affiliated with me.

Give me one word that sums up your life journey thus far: Exciting

What is the meaning of life?

God put the whole thing into motion so he could have a people of his own to worship and glorify him and to spend eternity with Him. He has been good to his people by bestowing his tender mercies and loving kindnesses on them.

Name: Caribbean Queen

Age: 43

Gender: Female

Country: UK

Occupation: Office Manager

Do you believe in God?

Not sure. I'd like to. Deep down God probably isn't 'real' however I do believe in spirituality.

What is the worst thing you've ever done?

Cheat on a partner.

What is your greatest achievement?

My son.

Tell me a secret about you:

I've had payday loans in the past. Only one other person knows. It's humiliating really.

If you could go back in time to age 20 with your current life experience, what would you do differently?

Start saving. Now!

There is a 15 year old standing in front of you. What life advice would you give him/her?

Get a part time job.

When you are an elderly person, sitting in your rocking chair and you look back on your life, what do you want to have achieved?

Bringing up my son to be a fine young man with a good job that earns him good money.

Give me one word that sums up your life journey thus far: Hectic!

What is the meaning of life?

Loving and being loved.

Name: Johnny Lyle

Age: 52

Gender: Male

Country: UK

Occupation: Marketing Director across a number of different businesses.

Do you believe in God?

No. We were bought up as strict (Irish) Catholics but when a priest put his hand on my arse when I was about 13, I have never been back in a church since other than for the odd funeral. My kids haven't been christened and I was married in a C of E church.

What is the worst thing you've ever done?

Maybe not the worst, but certainly one I regret the most, I took a load of speed to help me stay up all night to revise for my maths A level. I failed it.

What is your greatest achievement?

Walking again after breaking my back with a spinal Tumour.

Tell me a secret about you:

I lost my virginity when I was on a catholic retreat. We used to be sent away every summer to learn more about our religion. In three years I smoked (age 11) took speed (age 12) and lost my virginity (age 13). Not sure that was what my parents had in mind.

If you could go back in time to age 20 with your current life experience, what would you do differently?

Not much to be honest. By 20 I had already failed my A levels and lost my place at LSE and had started to get my life back on track having given up drink and drugs.

There is a 15 year old standing in front of you. What life advice would you give him/her?

Never stop learning and listening to people with different experiences to you.

Sometimes older people are right and can teach you something if you listen

Don't ever start smoking as it will be with you for life and will kill you

There is NO short cut to getting rich. A few are lucky, but in the main it's about learning and working

You can only spend it once

When you are an elderly person, sitting in your rocking chair and you look back on your life, what do you want to have achieved?

To have inspired people to achieve what they are capable of.

Give me one word that sums up your life journey thus far: Changeable.

What is the meaning of life?

I have to quote Stephen Covey here as his book (seven habits of highly effective people) has been very influential "To Live, love and leave a legacy."

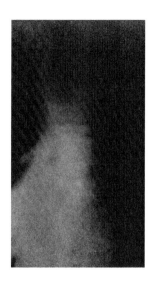

Name: Pauline Straw – my alter ego!

Age: 57

Gender: Female

Country: UK

Occupation: Regional Sales Manager

Do you believe in God?

Not sure about this one…only discussed it yesterday with my sister! It just doesn't seem possible logically but when I think of how we got here in the first place, that is so phenomenal; I think there must be something out there!

What is the worst thing you've ever done?

The worst thing I've ever done is cheat on a partner – it was so so destructive!

What is your greatest achievement?

Getting to 57!

Tell me a secret about you:

It won't be a secret if I tell you, silly, but genuinely, I don't have any! Except for this: Nobody at work knows I'm gay.

If you could go back in time to age 20 with your current life experience, what would you do differently?

Tell my parents I'm gay.

There is a 15 year old standing in front of you. What life advice would you give him/her?

Live your life honestly.

When you are an elderly person, sitting in your rocking chair and you look back on your life, what do you want to have achieved?

A life of honesty.

Give me one word that sums up your life journey thus far: Happy

What is the meaning of lifc?

An adventure.

Name: Jonathan Schneider

Age: 44

Gender: Male

Country: United States

Occupation: God

Do you believe in God?

I do believe in God, for it is by His grace that I am saved.

What is the worst thing you've ever done?

The worst thing that I have ever done, now I realize, is not having God in my life and going down the road of the devil. By doing this I constantly hurt others and always thought I was in control. I lost my wife in 2012 by divorce and my kids also.

What is your greatest achievement?

Accepting Jesus into my life and turning my will over to Him.

Tell me a secret about you:

I was into drugs and alcohol so bad that I lost total control. My friends didn't want me around, nor did my family. I lost numerous jobs and eventually ended up in prison in 2016.

If you could go back in time to age 20 with your current life experience, what would you do differently?

Really, I could think of a whole lot, but truthfully as much as I would want to change things, I wouldn't because I wouldn't be the man I am today. For God knew me before I was born and knew every move I would make. He used my bad experiences to make me stronger and a better man. For instance, I don't think I'd ever be writing this if it weren't for my past.

Romans 6:6 *"That our old self was crucified with Him, so that the body ruled by sin might be done away with, that we should no longer be slaves of sin. For he who died has been freed from sin"* By doing this I was transformed by the renewing.

For now not only having the Holy Spirit in me but also by being a doer of the word I am able not only to help myself but others.

There is a 15 year old standing in front of you. What life advice would you give him/her?

The advice I would give is that Jesus died on the cross and washed away our sins and by His blood we are cleansed. I would give my testimony of where I've been and how God has totally changed my life in hopes to bring them to the Lord.

When you are an elderly person, sitting in your rocking chair and you look back on your life, what do you want to have achieved?

I would like to have achieved helping others to Christ and having a family that serves the Lord.

Give me one word that sums up your life journey thus far: Servant

What is the meaning of life?

The meaning of life for me is being happy and joyous through all circumstances and bringing it to others. I know that I can't do this alone and need to have others walking down the same path. FOR Psalm133 says, *"Behold, how good and how pleasant it is for brethren to dwell together in unity! It is like the precious oil upon the head, that ran down upon the beard, even Aaron's beard, that went down to the skirts of his garments. As the dew of Hermon, and as the dew that descended upon the mountains of Zion: for there the Lord commanded the blessing: Life for evermore."*

I know that with God all things are possible.

Matthew 19:26 : *With men this is impossible, but with God all things are possible"* Amen. I give God all the glory and praise Him because I can do nothing without Him.

Name: Jenni
Age: 49
Gender: Female
Country: UK
Occupation: Security Officer

Do you believe in God?

I believe in God - a higher power timeless - the I am

What is the worst thing you've ever done?

Judged people when I was younger with my immature experience.

What is your greatest achievement?

My children for sure.

Tell me a secret about you:

I sold my ex husband's wedding ring when I found it on the floor as he was annoying me - big time . He lost it a few times so I thought I'd get some money for it. I got a lot of new outfits and wore them with pride. I left not long after and he never knew; not unless he reads this .....

If you could go back in time to age 20 with your current life experience, what would you do differently?

I would not judge anyone and follow my heart and do what I love. I would not put on a false front to please people and just be myself.

There is a 15 year old standing in front of you. What life advice would you give him/her?

I would say to them love yourself and get to know yourself - have a romance with yourself first and foremost then you will be ready for your life partner/soulmate to enter your life. Be kind and be grateful for everything.

When you are an elderly person, sitting in your rocking chair and you look back on your life, what do you want to have achieved?

To love and to have been loved and to have made a difference in people s life . To have given my sons stability self esteem and confidence.

Give me one word that sums up your life journey thus far: Gratitude

What is the meaning of life?

Reaching enlightenment through a spiritual awakening.
The Kingdom of God is within you ...

Name: Karl

Age: 42

Gender: Male

Country: United Kingdom

Occupation: Unemployed, but trained as an electrician

Do you believe in God?

I do believe in Gods, but also Goddesses. As a Pagan I believe in a nature based religion, where the forests and woodland are my church.

What is the worst thing you've ever done?

I regret the scare I gave my mum when I was younger. I went to the pub with a mate, got drunk, came home and during the night let myself out of the house and went for a walk. Mum woke in the morning to find my bed empty, and she rang the police. I arrived back home later as she was giving the police a description of me.

What is your greatest achievement?

My children are my greatest achievement and my proudest.

Tell me a secret about you:

Aged 18, I was working away from home, I got so drunk that I wet the bed and to avoid telling the hotel staff what had happened, I signed out of the hotel using my work mates hotel room number and signed him out in mine, so that they would think he had been in the messed room.

If you could go back in time to age 20 with your current life experience, what would you do differently?

I don't think that I would do anything differently, because I am a product of my experiences and I quite like the person I am.

There is a 15 year old standing in front of you. What life advice would you give him/her?

Don't be too hasty in leaving school or college, and don't rush into a job without thinking about it. Enjoy life, because it goes by in a flash and you don't want to miss a thing.

When you are an elderly person, sitting in your rocking chair and you look back on your life, what do you want to have achieved?

I would like to be the sort of person who people look at and think, he was a good person, a role model and kind.

Give me one word that sums up your life journey thus far: Bumpy

What is the meaning of life?

Love is all you need.

Name: Jenny Mitchell

Age: 60

Gender: Female

Country: UK, England

Occupation: Early retired/ Events - Murder Mystery - organiser

Do you believe in God?

Not at all. Never done me or many others any favours and too many wars caused in the name of religion. I also have found that 'Church' people are not always the nicest folk!

What is the worst thing you've ever done?

Difficult to share that/those, so I won't. I can talk about those decisions made that turned out to be the wrong ones. That comes later...

What is your greatest achievement?

Returning to University as a mature student and single mum of three children and achieving 2(i) in French Studies after 4 years of study, including four months spent studying at a French University near the Pyrenees.

Tell me a secret about you:

I tend to wear my heart on my sleeve, so not many secrets. I have especially nice breasts and nipples, or so I've been told. Will that do?

If you could go back in time to age 20 with your current life experience, what would you do differently?

I would drop my current (at age 20) boyfriend and hope to find a different partner who would be faithful throughout our relationship. I would study and work harder towards a career, although I would still want to have children in my twenties. (But then my kids wouldn't be the same, so maybe not!) I would be more adventurous and travel more, perhaps work abroad in my twenties. I would also be more careful with money, but hopefully be more able to enjoy the good things in life with my improved earning capacity. I'd make sure I had my own home from an early age for security later on, having been made effectively homeless twice in my life.

There is a 15 year old standing in front of you. What life advice would you give him/her?

Work hard, put in all the effort you can to what you do. But mostly be thoughtful and kind.

When you are an elderly person, sitting in your rocking chair and you look back on your life, what do you want to have achieved?

Some happiness, and having brought up my four sons to be adults I'm proud of.

Give me one word that sums up your life journey thus far: Complicated

What is the meaning of life?

There isn't a meaning, but I feel that while we are here it is important to be supportive and kind to others and helpful when one can.

Having children, bringing them up, has been the most wonderful part of my life.

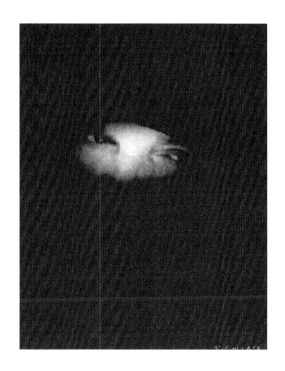

Name: Mr. Interiority

Age: …on the young side of being old.

Gender: I'm a male…

Country: United States of America

Occupation: Starving artist (voice actor), caregiver, guitar teacher, substitute teacher, semi-retired philosopher.

Do you believe in God?

I avoid the word "believe". I don't know if God is, or isn't. There seems to be a consciousness within all creation that operates outside human perception. We are constrained by the limitations of our senses – seeing and hearing a very limited rage of frequencies and wavelengths. This means that we do not know reality. Given that is the nature of things, my mind is open to possibilities; including the possibility of God. We live on a planet that appears miraculous to the eyes and sensibilities. I see an order and intelligence to creation that strikes me as indicative of there being something greater than just the random behavior of physical matter.

What is the worst thing you've ever done?

I shot a squirrel once with a BB gun. I always regretted that and have never done anything like it since. I don't even like to fish… poor fish - hook lodged in its mouth.

I snitched some coins from my neighbor's piggy bank when I was about 10 years old. I was damn sneaky. I wanted those candy bars from the vending machine. But I betrayed my neighbor's trust to get them. I had an ability to rationalize wrong doing ("oh, it won't hurt them financially.. it's just 75 cents"). I always felt bad about it. I did tell them many years later. I've worked to overcome that penchant for certain bad behaviors. I now abide by karmic principles because it really does seem that the bad stuff I've done has come around to kick my ass.

Regrets? I've had a few. But then again too many to mention. In hindsight, I might have avoided certain people and certain situations that occurred in my life had I known where they would ultimately take me.

There are jobs I left that, had I known how things would pan out going forward, I would not have left.

The things that I'm sad about, or regretful of, or ashamed of are little things. But yes, there have been more than a few.

What is your greatest achievement?

My daughter. And my house is paid off.

Tell me a secret about you:

Can you keep a secret?

Yeah?

So can I.

Next.

If you could go back in time to age 20 with your current life experience, what would you do differently?

Totally score babes. I'm now armed with extremely dangerous knowledge about how the game of love is truly played. In my youth I had it all wrong. Now I'm too old to enjoy my newfound awareness. But seriously, I might have gone ahead and taken more chances. I might not have played things as safe as I did.

There is a 15 year old standing in front of you. What life advice would you give him/her?

"Don't worry about things that haven't happened." Incredibly hard to not do, but that's my number one piece of advice. Otherwise, I've assembled a list of things that I've learned; things that I've come to believe are true and things that would qualify as advice to a youth. But, I'm not gonna share them here. They may end up as part of a book I wanna write. If I ever get around to it.

When you are an elderly person, sitting in your rocking chair and you look back on your life, what do you want to have achieved?

I think fear has held me back in life. I'd like to overcome it, but I don't think I've made a lot of progress in that regard. And it's getting late. Otherwise, I just want to break even. I'm not too terribly concerned about material achievements; they don't matter. I hope I've made people feel loved. I know I've been loved. And ultimately, I don't place too much emphasis on a single incarnation.

Give me one word that sums up your life journey thus far: Weird

What is the meaning of life?

To learn to expand the ability to love.

Name: Liberty Singer

Age: 45

Gender: Female

Country: England

Occupation: Choir Director/Vocal Coach

Do you believe in God?

Yes – yet I would not consider myself religious.

What is the worst thing you've ever done?

Went out with a guy (as friends because I already had a boyfriend) then got off with someone else. I was young. But I'm still not proud.

What is your greatest achievement?

My children.

From a work perspective, my greatest achievement is that I am able to reach out to people through singing and choirs and create communities full of good and happiness. I can build confidence and self esteem and provide the creative outlet so many people need in their busy lives.

Tell me a secret about you:

I have an unrequited desire to sing in a band.

If you could go back in time to age 20 with your current life experience, what would you do differently?

I would believe in myself more, trust my own opinions and not try so hard to please others and fit in.

There is a 15 year old standing in front of you. What life advice would you give him/her?

Believe in yourself. Have pride in yourself. Look to yourself for inspiration and motivation. Be yourself.

When you are an elderly person, sitting in your rocking chair and you look back on your life, what do you want to have achieved?

That my children have grown up fair and kind, happy and fulfilled and are able to live their lives honestly.

Give me one word that sums up your life journey thus far: Colourful

What is the meaning of life?

To achieve success and happiness, in whatever form that may take.

Name: LSP
Age: 52
Gender: Male
Country: US/UK
Occupation: Contractor

Do you boliovo in God?
Yes.

What is the worst thing you've ever done?
Bullied a kid at boarding school.

What is your greatest achievement?

Walking the Ten Tors and coming in ahead of the Royal Marines.

Tell me a secret about you:

I don't like killing animals.

If you could go back in time to age 20 with your current life experience, what would you do differently?

Go to RMA Sandhurst and NOT make ill considered, immature, stupid marriages.

There is a 15 year old standing in front of you. What life advice would you give him/her?

Work hard, be yourself, make your bed, don't whine and go at it 100% and then some. No one owes you anything.

When you are an elderly person, sitting in your rocking chair and you look back on your life, what do you want to have achieved?

Love.

Give me one word that sums up your life journey thus far: Adventure

What is the meaning of life?

To love, worship, adore and know God.

If you meet an Angel on the road, obey it.

Name: Felinity

Age: 64

Gender: Female

Country: USA

Occupation: Retired. Now volunteering and ministering in nursing homes and senior care centers.

Do you believe in God?

Yes.

What is the worst thing you've ever done?

This will be revealed to me when I stand before the Lord. After all, during our walk on earth, we weak, finite humans often find ways to close our eyes to – or explain away — the worst in ourselves.

What is your greatest achievement?

Having had the eyes of my heart opened – through elective Grace — to acknowledge and seek after God, Creator and Master of the Universe.

Tell me a secret about you:

None. But if I ever *thought* I harbored secrets no one would ever know, I'd be deluding myself, since God knows my heart…and knows me inside and out. Psalm 139 opens with: "*O LORD, You have searched me and known me.*" I often inwardly recite these words from Psalm 19:4: "*Let the words of my mouth and the meditation of my heart be acceptable in your sight, O LORD, my rock and my redeemer.*"

If you could go back in time to age 20 with your current life experience, what would you do differently?

Live life and derive delight in and from it by looking upward and outward. This realization came to me over several years as I gradually gained Wisdom (whose voice is continually hoarse from crying out in the streets for people to heed her—Prov. 1:20) about the fact that *life is all-encompassing; it's not just about each of us alone.*

There is a 15 year old standing in front of you. What life advice would you give him/her?

Take away the Smartphone, pull out the ear buds, and tell him/her #5…infused with the Gospel… then pray for him/her.

When you are an elderly person, sitting in your rocking chair and you look back on your life, what do you want to have achieved?

Heaven after life on earth, including said rocking chair.

Give me one word that sums up your life journey thus far: Blessed!

What is the meaning of life?

Our chief end is to glorify God and enjoy Him forever. Dietrich Bonhoeffer wrote: "…It is only by living completely in this world that one learns to have faith. One must completely abandon any attempt to make something of oneself, whether it be a saint, or a converted sinner or a churchman (a so-called priestly type!), a righteous or an unrighteous man, a sick man or a healthy man. By this-worldliness, I mean living unreservedly in life's duties, problems, successes and failures, experiences and perplexities. By living in this way, we throw ourselves completely into the arms of God, taking seriously not our own sufferings, but those of the God-man in the world — watching with Christ in Gethsemane. That, I think, is faith."

Name: Call me Ishmael

Age: I am *ugh* years old

Gender: I'm a man, yes I am and I can't help but love you so.

Country: USA

Occupation: Graphic design

Do you believe in God?

God is a man-made contrivance. I want to say yes because that's how I was raised and I'm afraid to say no. But I look around at the pain, violence and anger that's perpetrated in His name and I simply can't believe there's a God. Pay a visit to a paediatric burn unit and afterwards try to convince me there's a God.

What is the worst thing you've ever done?

My best friend married someone much, much older than he is. Believe me, he could've done better. She and I never got along. We competed for his attention and circled each other warily in the classic best friend/wife push/pull contest. She had a daughter who came to New York to go to college. I seduced her. After it came to light, he never spoke to me again.

What is your greatest achievement?

I rose above my station in life. I was dealt a weak hand. No father. No college. No guidance of any kind. The people who are charged with shepherding a child through the labyrinths looked at me like I was a vapor that somehow got into the room. But I built a life in New York City. Mastered the terrain and its ways. Discovered art, theater and music. Read voraciously and educated myself. I was able to make a comfortable, albeit modest, living and lead a much more interesting life than I thought I was capable of.

Tell me a secret about you:

I've had very little sex. Hardly any at all, really. I talk a good game and clean-up pretty well. Women have seduced me. But I always felt so unworthy of their affection and was so certain they'd find out what a fraud I was—that I'm not who I appeared to be—that I was rarely able to perform. I was overwhelmed with anxiety. This went on for decades.

If you could go back in time to age 20 with your current life experience, what would you do differently?

I'd find a way to go to college. If all you have is a high school diploma, no one will hire you, pretty girls will not kiss you and you are never taken seriously. You're put into a tiny box and very few people are willing to let you out. When I hear people disparage their college education, complain they never use their degree, I want to smack them. Remove that 'unused' degree from your resume and try to find work. Let me know how that goes. Plus, I missed out on the social growth that occurs organically in that environment. College is a common experience. A slender, silver thread that runs through everyone's life. It can be the cornerstone of lifelong friendships. I missed out on that.

There is a 15 year old standing in front of you. What life advice would you give him/her?

Don't waste your time doing boring work. Chase something. And I don't mean money. If things don't work out, then chase money. Eventually, you have to pay the bills. But don't be so consumed with fear and doubt that you never attempt the impossible. It probably won't work out—it doesn't for the vast majority of us—but you must *try*. You *must*.

When you are an elderly person, sitting in your rocking chair and you look back on your life, what do you want to have achieved?

The greatest thing you'll ever learn

Is just to love and be loved in return

eden ahbez

Give me one word that sums up your life journey thus far: Inadvertent

What is the meaning of life?

Mankind's greatest philosophers and theologians haven't sufficiently answer this question. How do you expect us to? It's contingent upon your individual life's experience and no two people have walked the exact same path. It's unanswerable.

Name: Laurie Murray

Age: 70

Gender: Female

Country: USA

Occupation: Book Keeper / Pastoret

Do you believe in God?

Yes, just look around, God is everywhere.

What is the worst thing you've ever done?

looked for love in wrong places because of being hurt by others.

What is your greatest achievement?

Being a child of God.

Tell me a secret about you:

I tried to end my life at age 12.

If you could go back in time to age 20 with your current life experience, what would you do differently?

I'd hopefully not make so many wrong decisions.

There is a 15 year old standing in front of you. What life advice would you give him/her?

Enjoy life, remember right from wrong, respect elders and yourself.

When you are an elderly person, sitting in your rocking chair and you look back on your life, what do you want to have achieved?

Making a difference in someone else's life.

Give me one word that sums up your life journey thus far: Crazy

What is the meaning of life?

To be a light in this dark world.

Name: Mark Stafford

Age: 60

Gender: Male

Country: England

Occupation: Engineer

Do you believe in God?

No.

What is the worst thing you've ever done?

Lied to my mother that I was staying at my dad's when she went on a weeks holiday. I had a week long party and the house was wrecked. She never forgot - lived till she was 85 and still mentioned it.

What is your greatest achievement?

Having 3 wonderful children.

Tell me a secret about you:

I cant keep a secret so I have no secrets.

If you could go back in time to age 20 with your current life experience, what would you do differently?

If I could return to age of 20 I would hopefully not waste time learning how not to do things.

There is a 15 year old standing in front of you. What life advice would you give him/her?

Get qualified in any career that will guarantee you work, then do what you want.

When you are an elderly person, sitting in your rocking chair and you look back on your life, what do you want to have achieved?

Enjoyed life and not upset anyone on the way.

Give me one word that sums up your life journey thus far: Okay

What is the meaning of life?

Still looking.

Name: Lisa ward

Age: 35

Gender: Female

Country: United Kingdom

Occupation: Exhibitions Curator

Do you believe in God?

Yes, although I have always connected with God through the green spaces, nature. I do occasionally go to church, and love the community, the collective energy there, but I usually find God in the quiet places.

What is the worst thing you've ever done?

I was in a relationship, and generally felt unhappy, but wasn't sure why. I was depressed, but then seeing my boyfriend I put that aside and put on my happy face. So much so I could kid myself into believing I was happy at those times. I lied to him about how bad things were. He realised things were wrong with me, so much so he suggested we finish the relationship if it would help me. His offer touched me so much I decided it must be worth persevering with, but I should have accepted instead.

Eventually I broke down, said I couldn't do it any more. I didn't know if it was something about me, something about him, something about us, I just didn't feel like I could handle a relationship and whatever else was going on with me. Because I'd not been honest to him, it felt like a shock, the severity, the sudden change in me, the fact there was no fixing things. I just needed out.

Sometimes, what seems like the easy route in life causes much more pain down the line.

What is your greatest achievement?

When in high school I went to an after school club for drama. We were in our GCSE years and we found out that the club for younger students would be finishing as there weren't teachers available or willing to provide it. A couple of friends and I decided to run the club, all it would need is a teacher to be present.

We put on a slightly rubbish end of year show in assembly, but the students in the club all seemed to love their time there (well, they kept coming back!) A friend and I were awarded school colours to thank us for our services to Drama.

I recently found out, that about 20 years later, the club is still going, and running it is still being handed down from student group to student group. I'm so proud that we started something from which 11 to 14 year olds are benefiting from, run by 15 to 17 year olds who also benefit from their experience.

Tell me a secret about you:

I spend a lot of time convinced someone is about to call me out on not really doing what I should be, and that I'm just good at looking effective.

If you could go back in time to age 20 with your current life experience, what would you do differently?

Well, see that big mistake above with the relationship… I'd try and get out of bad situations when I realise they are bad, not keep trying to fix things, or being in denial.

There is a 15 year old standing in front of you. What life advice would you give him/her?

Most adults are just mentally still somewhere around 19, with an internal mix of confidence, panic and bewilderment about the life situations they now find themselves in.

Adults don't have the answers, there's no fantastic moment where you become wise, and they are just as prone to monumental cock ups as anyone. It's just they often have more experience at looking calm and collected as they get through the consequences, and more resources to call upon to get them out of the situation.

The most difficult thing you may need to do is break up with a friend. We are shown and taught by society how to break up a romantic relationship, but realising when a toxic friend should no longer be in your life is difficult, and getting distance without appearing to be an arse about it is hard, if not impossible.

Any big decision you make will be the best one you can make at the time, with the information you have to hand. Later you will probably second guess, doubt, perhaps regret, but try to remember that you decided what was right at the time.

If you do the wrong thing, or what you think is right but there are bad consequences. Learn from it. Don't spiral around being angry, depressed, in denial. Go through those emotions and then look at what, why, your processes, talk to people, and then package it up, and only take away with you what you need to do next time.

When you are an elderly person, sitting in your rocking chair and you look back on your life, what do you want to have achieved?

I want as few people as possible to have been inconvenienced by me, and those I have met to have warm memories.

I don't need a big blood related family around me, but to know that I've made other connections in small ways.

Give me one word that sums up your life journey thus far: Agh!

What is the meaning of life?

Try and leave things better than you found them.

Name: Mark Williams

Age: 40

Gender: Male

Country: UK

Occupation: Business Development Director

Do you believe in God?

I don't personally believe in a physical entity or share many culture's interpretations of how the World begun, however, I also cannot accept that after life there is nothing and that our loved ones simply cease to exist. If i'm honest, I'm not sure where the distinction is between what I 'know' to be true and what I want to believe.

What is the worst thing you've ever done?

The worst thing i've ever done is a strange one as the answer would be in the eye of the beholder although If I had to share the one thing which I regret more than any other is, then it would be not being able to speak at my mum's funeral and share my experiences with loved ones. I feel I let her down by not doing so and perhaps showed her a lack of respect by letting the priest (a stranger) read my memories on my behalf. On a lighter note, I am sure the worst is yet to come.

What is your greatest achievement?

I know it's a cliche, however, my greatest achievement are my kids. Not in having them but in raising them well, with my wife, wider family and friends, to be the amazing young people they have become. I am so proud of them and work hard to give them every experience life can throw at them.

Tell me a secret about you:

I had the hottest babysitter when I was young and you might even say I had a little crush on her ;)

If you could go back in time to age 20 with your current life experience, what would you do differently?

I have made many mistakes but I wouldn't change a thing. To do so would risk not meeting my wife, not having my kids or maybe not even being here. Ive read too many books and seen too many sci-fi films to believe changing something would not have an impact on future events.

There is a 15 year old standing in front of you. What life advice would you give him/her?

University in the UK is now so expensive and every man and his dog has a qualification so, if you have chosen to go to uni, give yourself the best opportunity to stand out from the crowd and go to university overseas and double your experience and education. Im not saying go to Australia or the States but become fluent in a second language, learn a new culture, meet great people and do what much of the rest of the world do. Become truly international.

When you are an elderly person, sitting in your rocking chair and you look back on your life, what do you want to have achieved?

I would like to be remembered by many people as a good person and to have had a positive impact on others' lives. I would also want my kids to think of me as a great dad. Ideally I would be sitting on the deck of my super-yacht off the coast of Italy surrounded by my family whilst reminiscing.

Give me one word that sums up your life journey thus far: Spicy

What is the meaning of life?

I would simply say that it is to take the biggest evolutionary step forward possible. My kids are fitter, brighter and better people than I am and I know that when the time comes, they will also make great parents. The meaning of my life is to give them the opportunities that enable them to take the next giant leap forwards.

Everything said, you may as well be happy whilst living life so have fun and enjoy yourself. By not doing so would be disrespectful to those who have come before.

Name: Matahari

Age: 68

Gender: Female

Country: England

Occupation: Retired

Do you believe in God?

Yes I believe there is a greater entity and faith keeps me strong.

What is the worst thing you've ever done?

Trashed and wrecked a bus shelter with friends when I was a teenager.

What is your greatest achievement?

My child and her children seeing the generations and family tree move into the future.

Tell me a secret about you:

Very few people know but I had a child out of wedlock as a teenager and he was adopted.

If you could go back in time to age 20 with your current life experience, what would you do differently?

Absolutely nothing I used to think that changing things would be great but I am a fatalist and I think that our life experiences are what make us the person that we are and what we do in life is a path chosen by ourselves.

There is a 15 year old standing in front of you. What life advice would you give him/her?

I would say follow your heart and your dream but remember to take your brain with you to balance your actions.

When you are an elderly person, sitting in your rocking chair and you look back on your life, what do you want to have achieved?

To have loved and been loved. To have shared and understood other cultures. To leave a generation of my mad genes to rock the world.

Give me one word that sums up your life journey thus far: Wow

What is the meaning of life?

You get one chance, grab it, get out there, enjoy it and live life to the full, never be afraid to give your heart and soul if you get hurt you will still live to love another day.

Never intentionally hurt another person We are all somewhat intolerant and say and do things in anger but deliberate cruelty is unforgivable.

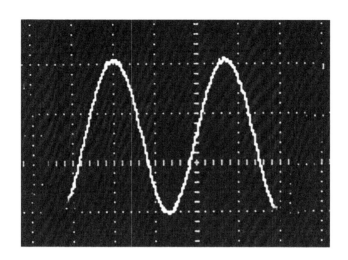

Name: Masher

Age: Getting on

Gender: I'm a man

Country: Albion

Occupation: Occupied

Do you believe in God?

No.

To paraphrase Woody Allen: I'm what you would call a teleological existential atheist. I don't believe in God, but I do believe there's an intelligence to the universe... with the exception of certain parts of Stoke Newington.

What is the worst thing you've ever done?

Depends on what you define as "worst". Unlike our Prime Minister, I've never done anything quite as heinous as running through a field of wheat, but, in my 56 years, I daresay I have committed a few odious acts.

A memory that occasionally troubles me, is from when we were kids - young teenagers - and one boring summer we befriended an old lady. For the life of me, I can't think how or why this happened, or how an old girl in her eighties would allow three young Herbert's into her home. But she did. I think she just wanted some company.

Of course, we thought it was great, being in somebody's house, when we knew that we probably shouldn't be there. We visited her several times and she would make us milk lollies - which were horrible - and tell us stories about the war. Thinking back, maybe she didn't quite have all her marbles.

She had a cat though and whilst she was talking to us in her living room, Col would terrorise the cat out in the hallway, trying to get it so scared that it would shit itself on the carpet. Which it did. Several times. I was never a cat fan, even back then, but I could never abide animal cruelty, so I kept away.

One day, the old lady left her purse on the sideboard, so Baz and Col saw this as an open invitation to nick her money. I think they took several pounds each.

I didn't take anything. Honestly.

After stealing her money, we never went back.

So, why do I consider this a contender for the worst thing I have ever done? I didn't steal her money. I didn't kick her cat.

But, my mates did and I should have said something. But I didn't.

I sometimes drive past that old lady's house today, over forty years later, and I still feel a pang of guilt.

What is your greatest achievement?

Beating my son at Mario Kart after about 200 attempts, ranks quite highly.

Tell me a secret about you:

I love magic. Not magic as in the occult and witches and shit like that, but magic as in conjuring and illusions. I'm addicted to magic shows on the TV and love Dynamo and David Blaine (back when he did proper street magic and not just sitting in a suspended perspex box), Penn & Teller and the late, great Paul Daniels, who was an incredibly talented , but seriously underestimated, magician. I've studied magic for over thirty years and have bought many tricks from various purveyors.

And - with the exception of a few card tricks - I've never shown them to anybody, for fear that my performance won't be good enough and I'll inadvertently reveal how it's done.

But, from the very few card tricks that I have mastered and shown, I've got immense pleasure… seeing that look of wonder, bafflement and delight on someone's face when you make an impossible reveal, can be most gratifying.

If you could go back in time to age 20 with your current life experience, what would you do differently?

I remember Sir Benjamin Britten (I think it was) being asked a similar question, when he was old and wheelchair bound, and my answer is much the same as he gave: I'd probably have more sex!

You see, I was frightfully shy as a teenager and even well into my twenties.

There were girls that I fancied (there were even girls who made it known that they fancied me), but talking to them in any way other than polite conversation, was just not possible for me.

It took a long time to get the courage up to ask someone out for the first time.

But, once I did, after that there was no stopping me :)

I've always been annoyed at myself for all those 'lost years'.

There is a 15 year old standing in front of you. What life advice would you give him/her?

Be yourself, would be one piece of advice I'd give.

Don't try to be like others, just to fit in.

And don't worry what others may think of you.

It's your life, so you live it how you want to.

Within reason.

When you are an elderly person, sitting in your rocking chair and you look back on your life, what do you want to have achieved?

Not a lot. I'd be happy just to know that I've provided well for my family; made some good friends, lived a full life and secured myself a quality rocking chair..

Give me one word that sums up your life journey thus far: Adequate

What is the meaning of life?

Love. Friendship. Humour.

Name: Classic Car Lady

Age: 70

Gender: Female

Country: England

Occupation: Retired. Previously employment restaurant manageress, team sales leader, retail trainer, training development manager, self employed antique dealer

Do you believe in God?

Yes.

What is the worst thing you've ever done?

I had a termination as I couldn't see how I could bring this child into a world it wouldn't be loved.

What is your greatest achievement?

I think to bring three daughters into the world and raise them to be considerate, hard working, happy people with families of their own despite a lot of problems we all experienced in their early lives.

Tell me a secret about you:

I would love to have been an actress.

If you could go back in time to age 20 with your current life experience, what would you do differently?

I would not get married as young as I did at 19yrs after very little life experience and being with the same partner for 4yrs, and I would travel more, and look to reach goals in life instead of accepting things.

There is a 15 year old standing in front of you. What life advice would you give him/her?

I should advise her to live life to the fullest without hurting people, always have goals to achieve and whatever you are doing ,do it to your best ability.

When you are an elderly person, sitting in your rocking chair and you look back on your life, what do you want to have achieved?

In years I suppose people think I'm not that far away from the rocking chair now but believe me I have no intention of giving up enjoying life for a long while yet! I hope when it is time for me to stop and look back at my life I hope that I can say I have made a lot of people happy, whether it was by being a good mum , grandma, friend or during my work with young people, I have helped them in their careers and I am appreciated.

Give me one word that sums up your life journey thus far: Unexpected

What is the meaning of life?

I think we should be nice to and love as many people as possible and be tolerant to those we can't like or love.

I think life gives you what you put into it so if you don't make any effort in life nothing can improve or change and in general most people will treat you with respect if you are nice to them. I do find nowadays though that a lot of the younger generation have no respect for anybody and I put that down to lack of proper parenting.

Name: Matt. Matthew if I've been naughty, else Matt. I'm not naughty. Just ask Santa.

Age: 43

Gender: Male

Country: England

Occupation: Software Developer.

Do you believe in God?

Which God? There are many to choose from but yet evidence for none. Believing in something without evidence is a slippery slope. Faith is in opposition to critical thinking and even if I thought that faith was a choice then I prize the latter too much to relinquish it.

What is the worst thing you've ever done?

I honestly can't thinking of anything. I wrote some graffiti on a pole once, but in my defence I was correcting some grammar (as I explained to the policeman).

What is your greatest achievement?

Max (son) turning out to be a decent human being (that and working out the mighty combination of a bowl of beans and slices of corned beef).

Tell me a secret about you:

I don't think I'll ever take a great photograph.

If you could go back in time to age 20 with your current life experience, what would you do differently?

Tell myself to invest in Apple shares.

There is a 15 year old standing in front of you. What life advice would you give him/her?

Earn enough to live the life you want. Don't follow trends. Don't try and fit in to be happy. Find something you're passionate about and follow it.

When you are an elderly person, sitting in your rocking chair and you look back on your life, what do you want to have achieved?

That I tried my best.

Give me one word that sums up your life journey thus far: Trying

What is the meaning of life?

Having Experiences.

A new question. What trivial thing annoys yo
it should?

more than

Name: Miss A

Age: 55

Gender: Female

Country: USA

Occupation: Writer and freelancer in all things publishing.

Do you believe in God?

Short answer: I believe in a higher power, HP, not the sauce.

My parents set the scene for belief in God—Sunday School and religious services at a Protestant church— but there are some abstract concepts one has to take to the open road to test. I headed down south at 20 with headspace for God only, so Jesus and the Holy Spirit were left to fend for themselves.

All told, it took a whole lot of hell-raising, 3 brushes with Death, a few awkward attempts at Being Someone, 2 years of intense Bible study, 4 new age spiritual paths, and countless answers to my desperate, heavenward pleas over a period of 39 years, to come to my current understanding that there is a higher power—call it God, Universe, Angels, what have you—that is all for us humans finding our way to living joyous, fulfilled lives. The timing of all the asking and answering is a mystery; for me it seems tied to being whipped enough to sit atop one of Life's desserts.

What is the worst thing you've ever done?

Short answer: I left a dog for a man and boy was I sorry!

I had a Zen Master called Nova who looked like a Lhasa Apso. He taught me how to properly treat dogs and all sentient beings. When he was 15, I fell in love with a man from another country. Perhaps it was the proposal of marriage that knocked Nova's teachings to the back of my head and made me feel a bit Disney™. I began preparing him for travel starting with an unpleasant battery of rabies shots before I realized he likely wouldn't survive transport. I left him with my mother and tried to do it all, to fly back and forth to see him as much as I could…but you can't do half-assed what's ultimately important to you…

Nova was almost 17 when I flew in to spend a week with him before our vet came to assist him to the afterlife. Holding him to the end I could still feel the presence of his strong little will which made me feel like a killer, not the lady with the lamp. Nova would have carried on forever if he could, and I would do his last years differently if I could.

Addendum: Over much time I assimilated the above experience as Nova's last lesson in which he taught me to seriously get a handle on who I am and what I value and to stand by that resolutely…because in the end I want to be sorry for as little as possible.

What is your greatest achievement?

Short answer: It's yet to come.

I'd started typing my hoity-toity party answer when it hit me hard that there was an unassuming yet *far* greater thing I did at a crossroads where I dared veer off the road of mediocrity toward creativity. And this departure led to the creation of Miss Alister and her short-lived Golden Age, the period of time in which I felt the most alive and electric.

I started a writing blog called The Essence of a Thing with intent to see if I was any good and if I was, to use it to get better and better, and Miss Alister came into her own. She was a mix of halves—the tortured artist and the moon controlling the tides, ingénue and femme-fatale, mad scientist and sage—all of which miraculously congealed to render a consistency of inspired, insightful, and witty writing.

There is a social media motto for her, "Ever planning the big comeback," but those are my words, not hers. Miss Alister will never be back as she was. No age can be identically recreated, but a new age based on an old one can be created. In that vein, I'm working at breathing the life of her into a novel based on one of her short stories that contained concepts needing much more space to explode into.

Tell me a secret about you:

The first of my three brushes with Death was a bang-up job of a suicide gone wrong at age 16. The other brushes were from doing dumb stuff I like to think I wouldn't have done had I not lost so many brain cells during the first brush! Making light aside, I feel like all the crazy stuff I ever did, deadly or not, was an integral part of the journey to the me that I'm meant to be.

If you could go back in time to age 20 with your current life experience, what would you do differently?

Short answer: Everything to do with predispositions and education.

My high school classmates and teachers knew more about my future than I did. The senior yearbook committee made predictions for each of us in the graduating class and I was predicted to become a best-selling novelist who writes exposés of small New England towns. A teacher entered an essay I'd written into a competition and I won. I barely remember those days, I was that detached. I was there because I was told to be and that is all.

So if, in the middle of hell-raising in Florida, I was struck with the knowing born of mega-years of grappling with life out of confusion, anger, and downright stupidity, I would first make haste to college. I'd go for a BA with an eye on an MFA. My life would be about writing: reading great writers' works and practicing writing every day until I embodied in voice and craft, the art and mystery of exceptional writing. If teaching middle school English didn't give me enough spare time to do that, I'd find a job that did.

There is a 15 year old standing in front of you. What life advice would you give him/her?

Short answer: "Low key, it can take minutes to years to know exactly what you're meant to be and do on this planet, but be Gucci, you'll find the answer if every day you be a lil extra and seek it."

—Sydney Hayden, Supreme Teen

Your decisions are powerful: You don't have to know exactly why you're here to make the decision to create a life for yourself in which you're doing the most excellent thing you do that brings you joy and fulfilment.

Be your best friend: Enough people on your journey are going to give you a hard time so make being with yourself a respite from that. Go over experiences, take away anything of value, decide what you will change. There are no mistakes, only lessons learned.

Hang with the right people: Mentors and like-minded friends give you knowledge and encouragement to get your life goals, so keep them close and ditch anyone who's a deterrent to you; *seriously*, drop them like hot potatoes, slam the door, cut the cord.

Stay true to yourself and your values: On the road of life learn who you *really* are—your Jekyll, your Hyde, your strengths, your limitations, what inspires you, what

pursuits fill you with joy, what means the utmost to you—
and let that be your guiding light.

When you are an elderly person, sitting in your rocking chair and you look back on your life, what do you want to have achieved?

Short answer: Having lived a great many years as a fully realized individual.

The rocking chair is on the porch of a modern log cabin overlooking a lake near a small, unbothered southern town. Supper's in the oven, my happy hour whiskey's in my hand, and I'm watching the gap close between the sun and the water. The chair's creaking runners beat a rhythm of memories like the wheels on my road trip with the HP kicking the back of my driver's seat.

When the sun splashes down and sinks, and the neon pinks and oranges barely begin to dull, I'll go inside and fix myself a plate. And if another tomorrow greets me, I'll get up and do what I've done for the last 20 sem-odd years: return my completed edits to the copyeditor for one novel and get back to work on my next novel. Nine of them and still counting. Not too shabby for a late start outta the gate.

Give me one word that sums up your life journey thus far: Anticipatory

What is the meaning of life?

Many religions have a theme of [God] seeing/experiencing life through the perspectives of every living being. If that's true, from my eyes the meaning of life might look and feel like a rabid urgency to find and walk the path that leads us to who we really are and what we feel we're meant to do during our time on Earth, i.e. to become fully realized persons, and to enjoy as many years as possible living our full potential of talents and abilities.

Aw but that's only because I got a late start and I know my life could be snuffed at any moment by anvils and pianos falling from the sky and such. But in a rare, laid-back state I might say that the meaning of life is to live out one's definition of the meaning of life…

Name: Mike_C

Age: You could say "50's" or "sixth decade of life" or "post-Sputnik".

Gender: cis-male

Country: United States

Occupation: Medical research

Do you believe in God?

No. Don't exactly disbelieve either. Agnostic, but convinced that if there is a Supreme Deity, and it is the psychotic from the Old Testament then we are well and truly fucked. I am extremely dubious about HDMs (hot-desert monotheism — my personal term for all the Abrahamic religions) in general.

What is the worst thing you've ever done?

Failed to support my mother as I should have after my father's stroke.

What is your greatest achievement?

Can't think of anything.

Tell me a secret about you:

I am a lazy underachiever (but that's not much of a secret)

If you could go back in time to age 20 with your current life experience, what would you do differently?

Would not waste all those years in grad school. Would be much bolder about putting myself on the line emotionally. Would go with more ID/Ego and less Super-Ego.

There is a 15 year old standing in front of you. What life advice would you give him/her?

Take your work seriously, but not yourself as the doer of that work. In other words, strive to do your best in all things, but try to keep your ego out of it. Pride in a job well done is appropriate and deserved, but arrogance is not, because arrogance keeps you from learning from mistakes. Also, accept correction gracefully, even — nay, especially — if the person doing that correction is an insecure little twit. On the other hand, don't let anyone walk all over you, and always stand up for the powerless. Mean what you say, else don't say it. Make few promises, but keep the ones you make, regardless of the price.

Finally, no one thing is so terrible that it will ruin your life, no matter how bleak things may look at the time. Have some fun and take reasonable chances.

When you are an elderly person, sitting in your rocking chair and you look back on your life, what do you want to have achieved?

Figuratively, to have planted and nurtured healthy and growing young trees, even though I will not live to sit under their shade.

Give me one word that sums up your life journey thus far: an UNPLANNED (there's your one word) jumble that could be better, but could be a hell of a lot worse. Lois McMaster Bujold has a line which is a little sad but appropriate: Most of the time it's stumbling around in the dark, bumping into things and wondering why it hurts.

What is the meaning of life?

There isn't one. We have to make it have meaning. (I know this sounds nihilistic and existential, but actually I think the opposite.)

Name: Natasha Toomey

Age: 37

Gender: Female

Country: UK

Occupation: Infant massage and infant yoga teacher/ Doula

Do you believe in God?

I think so..

What is the worst thing you've ever done?

Hurt someone's feelings deeply.

What is your greatest achievement?

My children x3

Tell me a secret about you:

I am still in love with my first love .

If you could go back in time to age 20 with your current life experience, what would you do differently?

Nearly everything, make less rash decisions and not cut mannose off to spite my face, save money, get on the property ladder.

There is a 15 year old standing in front of you. What life advice would you give him/her?

Be you, love you as no one will love you better. Be the best you can be

When you are an elderly person, sitting in your rocking chair and you look back on your life, what do you want to have achieved?

A happy healthy future for my children to have been the best mum I could be.

Have achieved enough to be proud of myself.

Bought my own home.

Travelled more.

To have loved and been loved.

Left a positive imprint on others.

Give me one word that sums up your life journey thus far: Curates egg

What is the meaning of life?

I'm still searching but I think it means to achieve whatever you can, grasp it with two hands we only get one chance (as far as I know!)

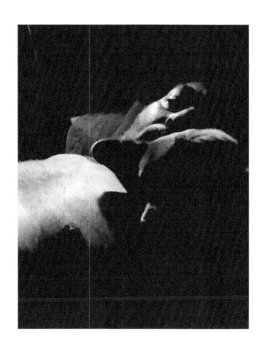

Name: Mike
Age: 60
Gender: Male
Country: USA
Occupation: Retired

Do you believe in God?
Absolutely!

What is the worst thing you've ever done?
That's between me and the Almighty.

What is your greatest achievement?

Raising a family.

Tell me a secret about you:

I covertly work with law enforcement whenever necessary.

If you could go back in time to age 20 with your current life experience, what would you do differently?

A lot. I'd be single without any family.

There is a 15-year-old standing in front of you. What life advice would you give him/her?

Work for your needs and strive, through hard work you get what you want. NOTHING is free and only what's earned is ever truly appreciated.

When you are an elderly person, sitting in your rocking chair and you look back on your life, what do you want to have achieved?

I wish we had stayed together, kept the farmland and built the cabins I had planned so we could live off the grid.

Give me one word that sums up your life journey thus far: Struggle

What is the meaning of life?

Biologically: To propagate and survive. Spiritually: To realize that our bodies are mere vessels and that our spirits are the true occupants, thereof.

Life is a fluid journey; there is no single "goal". Life is a series of steps, each a goal in and of itself. Take one step at a time and appreciate what you have. Rest. Then strive onward. Dream but do not pine for what's missing. Instead, be satisfied with what is tangibly yours. "You are where you are because you want to be". And, if not, change it.

Name: Chicken Pie

Age: 44

Gender: Female

Country: UK

Occupation: Support worker / team leader

Do you believe in God?

Yeah I do. The reason why is because this cannot just come from nowhere. All this feeling, love, emotion has to come from somewhere greater and more beautiful.

What is the worst thing you've ever done?

I think it's more to myself. Not honest and truthful to myself. I'm a coward to be honest, with my feelings and fears which has affected others. If you're not honest with yourself and afraid to be yourself then it has an impact on your relationships.

What is your greatest achievement?

My work that I'm doing now, working in mental health. Because you're giving back and that is a good thing. Also being consistent with my loyalty – I think that's an achievement.

Tell me a secret about you:

Once when I was in Brighton I got really wasted on all sorts and I got arrested and ended up in the cells. I was worried incase it went on my CRB record. I was off my rocker – didn't know where I lived or anything. I fucking hated it 'cos they woke me up every 20 mins to make sure I was OK and still alive. It was baltic cold in those cells.

If you could go back in time to age 20 with your current life experience, what would you do differently?

Studied more. Not wasted my time partying. Concentrated more on my future and been more honest with myself and people who care about me. I've wasted so many years fooling myself saying "tomorrow, tomorrow, tomorrow" when I should have done it 20 years ago.

There is a 15 year old standing in front of you. What life advice would you give him/her?

Be honest, be truthful to yourself and those who are important to you. Don't be discouraged by negativity if you have ambition. Aim for your dreams. Work hard. Better to have tried than to be full of regret. Stay safe. Be happy. Once you're happy within yourself it opens all the other doors.

When you are an elderly person, sitting in your rocking chair and you look back on your life, what do you want to have achieved?

That I would have finally made peace with myself and the most important people in my life. To know that I did my best and that I gave something back.

Give me one word that sums up your life journey thus far: OMG. (Fact.)

What is the meaning of life?

Oh My God. Experiencing the most amazing and beautiful things in life and the most tragic and vile things that life chucks at you and dealing with it. Being at peace with yourself. Being the best that you can be and learning – that's a big fat one. Not being afraid to be true to yourself whether its right wrong/ good bad, whatever.

What do you think other people think about you? I think it's important what they think because you can't walk this world alone. You need someone to tell you that you're OK, you're loved and you're going in the right direction. You need to have pride in yourself.

Name: Stray

Age: 66

Gender: Male

Country: UK

Occupation: Retired teacher

Do you believe in God?

No.

What is the worst thing you've ever done?

I was very rude about the physical appearance of a female member of staff to a class of students. I did it for cheap laughs. She broke down in tears in the staffroom after they repeated my comments to her. She felt humiliated, so did I. It taught me a lesson.

What is your greatest achievement?

Remaining married for 45 years and bringing up 2 considerate, independent and kind daughters.

Tell me a secret about you:

Since a rugby tackle when I was 17 I have had absolutely no sense of smell. It was an advantage when I was a teacher.

If you could go back in time to age 20 with your current life experience, what would you do differently?

More travelling when the world was a less dangerous place.

There is a 15 year old standing in front of you. What life advice would you give him/her?

Don't live your life on line. Be considerate. Notice nature.

When you are an elderly person, sitting in your rocking chair and you look back on your life, what do you want to have achieved?

To still be living independently.

Give me one word that sums up your life journey thus far: Easy

What is the meaning of life?

To experience the beauty of the world in as many ways as possible.

Deep within you know what is right and wrong. Try and do what is right.

Name: Altaira Sheran

Age: 56

Gender: Female

Country: Canada

Occupation: Crafter of wire jewellery

Do you believe in God?

I believe in a creator...the creator of all things - a higher intelligence.

What is the worst thing you've ever done?

Fooled around some with a guy who was getting married the next day!

What is your greatest achievement?

My two children.

Tell me a secret about you:

LOL....I'm actually an Angel in disguise, to help humanity and Gaia get rid of the darkness and evil that has permeated reality here.

If you could go back in time to age 20 with your current life experience, what would you do differently?

I wouldn't get married to the men I have already! I'd wait for the ONE with unconditional love.

There is a 15 year old standing in front of you. What life advice would you give him/her?

Don't follow the crowd. Be your own master of your ship. better to be a leader than a sheep. Don't allow peer pressure make you do something that you don't believe is right. Follow your gut instincts! They will never lead you wrong.

When you are an elderly person, sitting in your rocking chair and you look back on your life, what do you want to have achieved?

Peace on Earth and peace in my life.

Give me one word that sums up your life journey thus far: Enlightening and/or empowering.

What is the meaning of life?

To learn your lessons here well and to love everyone.

Be authentic...know yourself and be the best you, you can possibly be. Reality is only what you create by your thoughts...so think positive!

Name: Paul Kennedy

Age: 58

Gender: Male

Country: UK

Occupation: Aquatic Consultant / ex actor.

Do you believe in God?

No, as in so far as it's possible to know. I believe in the idea of gods, but not in the actuality of their existence.

What is the worst thing you've ever done?

I threw a stone across a school playground at a girl because she was " dirty and smelly". It hit her on the leg – causing her no small discomfort. I was about 8 or 9, I'm still not happy about it.

What is your greatest achievement?

To have loved, and been loved.

In terms of work/career etc.; to have been very good at what I do!

Tell me a secret about you:

I would have married her or anything she wanted, but she wouldn't let me ask.

If you could go back in time to age 20 with your current life experience, what would you do differently?

I would have worked harder at getting work and opportunities. There's more value in being talented and giving

People the chance to see it, than in assuming that talent is visible to all.

There is a 15 year old standing in front of you. What life advice would you give him/her?

Pay attention to everything and everyone that you encounter. Wisdom needs to be worked for, to be learnt. You

May not be able to become what you want to be, but you can become as good as possible at what and who you are. It's how you do, not what you do that defines you.

When you are an elderly person, sitting in your rocking chair and you look back on your life, what do you want to have achieved?

I would hope to be able to look back at a life where all my encounters were largely favourable, occasionally profitable and often comical.

Give me one word that sums up your life journey thus far: Laughter

What is the meaning of life?

Often answered , God or God I dunno.

Traditionally it's the question of meaning IN life that we ask, such as why are we here ? etc.

Simply(I use the word advisedly!). It is all, dependent on ones' fortunes, a happy or unhappy accident.

Sparks of joy, happiness seem to count most:

John McGovern lifting the European Cup.

Ireland beating the All Blacks in Dublin.

Taking a bow on stage to rapturous applause.

Getting a card or message from someone you thought had forgotten you.

To sum up:

How do we carry-on?

Take it easy, but don't take the piss!

Name: Betty
Age: Newly 43!
Gender: Female
Country: England
Occupation: Administrator

Do you believe in God?

Nope.

What is the worst thing you've ever done?

Leaving my ex-husband, the father of my eldest son, and causing my son to live in split homes.

What is your greatest achievement?

Carrying and giving birth to 2 gorgeous boys.

Tell me a secret about you:

I hide clothes that I've bought because I'm ashamed to spend money on myself.

If you could go back in time to age 20 with your current life experience, what would you do differently?

Worry less. Smile more. Not allow myself to be controlled by my Mum. Get away from being near my step dad and so my health didn't suffer as badly as it did. Tried to find a course I was interested in at uni, so I had a passion for what I was learning, or even, gone out and got a job instead of going to uni for my Mum. Took better control of my life. Not let people bully me, their opinions didn't matter! Stop being a people pleaser, see value in my own happiness. Focus on learning and friends rather than pursuing a partner in an attempt to complete my life! Travel!

There is a 15 year old standing in front of you. What life advice would you give him/her?

Focus on building a life and loving yourself a little bit. You don't need a boyfriend or girlfriend to complete you.

When you are an elderly person, sitting in your rocking chair and you look back on your life, what do you want to have achieved?

I would like to have found a job I enjoy doing. I'd like to have a good relationship with my sons. I'd like to have not fucked up this marriage and for us to still be madly in love.

Give me one word that sums up your life journey thus far: Rocky

What is the meaning of life?

To evolve to become a better person. To learn from mistakes and make better decisions. To leave people you've encountered, with a smile rather than a frown.

Name: Peter

Age: 62

Gender: Male

Country: USA

Occupation: Rancher/Contractor/Artisan/Full-time Handsome Cowboy

Do you believe in God?

Absolutely! I'm not religious but there's no denying God had a hand in everything. I'm outside 365 days a year and pay close attention to our natural world. None of it is an accident or coincidence.

What is the worst thing you've ever done?

It's classified.

What is your greatest achievement?

Good question… I've had many successes in life. From the time I was a small child I wanted to own a ranch and breed world class Quarter Horses. My dream was realized in my 30's. I've been living the dream ever since.

Tell me a secret about you:

It's classified.

If you could go back in time to age 20 with your current life experience, what would you do differently?

I should have married the love of my life. I was too young and too naive to see what was in front of me. My only regret.

There is a 15 year old standing in front of you. What life advice would you give him/her?

Work your butt off, do it well, be the best at what you do always and you will be noticed by those that can affect your life and you will be rewarded accordingly.

Be polite and respect others.

Be honest in all things.

Don't be a doormat for others.

Keep your promises. Always.

Stop talking and listen (especially to elders).

Look at people when speaking with them.

Never give up, especially your dreams.

Focus.

Listen to your inner voice, it's never wrong.

Ignore those that pull you down.

Don't do or tolerate drama and stay away from those who do.

Learn something new and interesting every day. Steal with your eyes and ears.

Don't follow your peers, be your own leader. Be the master of your own destiny.

Make friends with smart people.

Never make excuses. Own up to your mistakes and then learn from them.

Develop your skills then act and perform like a professional while continuously honing your skills and do this your whole life.

Stay away from college and universities as they are indoctrination centers. Go to a trade school.

Don't forget to laugh. Smile a lot. It's contagious.

Don't sweat the little stuff. It's just noise. Stay focused.

Honor your parents, your family, and your heritage.

Always be honorable, especially to your wife or husband.

Don't marry early but marry the love of your life. You'll know who he or she is. Never marry someone who does not have dreams that are incompatible with yours. Choose a propeller not an anchor.

When you are an elderly person, sitting in your rocking chair and you look back on your life, what do you want to have achieved?

Honestly, I am quite content already and have achieved everything I set out to do. God willing and the creek don't rise, I figure I have 20 good years left and still dream up stuff to do. That said, I want to be remembered as an honorable, hard working man that was good at his life's work, who made his own way in life, who had principles and lived by them, who made a difference, who was a good steward of the land, who was a true friend, and left behind a legacy that can be realized by others. In the end, I want to die with my boots on.

Give me one word that sums up your life journey thus far: Success

What is the meaning of life?

Happiness. Whatever one does they should be happy. If one does a job that is satisfying and brings happiness into their lives then you'll never work a day in your life. This is critical.

Live by your own personal constitution and be honest with yourself.

Name: Rosemary Moeckel

Age: 54

Gender: Female

Country: USA

Occupation: Escrow Officer – close real estate transactions

Do you believe in God?

Absolutely!

What is the worst thing you've ever done?

When I started thinking of this question, I got to thinking that I am a pretty good person! The worst thing I've done?

Accidentally - Wrecking my parents car. Purposefully –
skipping school.

What is your greatest achievement?

My family! My marriage, my children and my grandchildren
are my greatest and proudest achievement!

Tell me a secret about you:

If I tell you…. it won't be a secret anymore!

If you could go back in time to age 20 with your current life experience, what would you do differently?

I would get on anxiety medicine ASAP so I can enjoy my
life as it happens. I spent too much time worrying and not
enough enjoying. I would have started going to a church
where I got more out of the sermons and a church that
had a close family-type congregation. I would not spend
time in jobs that were miserable.

There is a 15 year old standing in front of you. What life advice would you give him/her?

Be your own person. Love yourself. Don't do ANYTHING
for others' approval. Don't try to please everyone, it never
works. Treat everyone with love and kindness. Find a job
you love! Find your passion! If you don't know Jesus,
invite Him into your heart now! He is the best friend you
will ever have!

When you are an elderly person, sitting in your rocking chair and you look back on your life, what do you want to have achieved?

LOVE! I want to love and be loved by my family, friends and church! Love is the only legacy you can leave!

Give me one word that sums up your life journey thus far: BLESSED!

What is the meaning of life?

Life is meant to be spent worshiping God and loving his people! Other than this, life is meaningless.

Name: Pete

Age: 58

Gender: Male

Country: England

Occupation: Artist

Do you believe in God?

I believe there is a higher power, yes. But what constitutes that I couldn't say.

What is the worst thing you've ever done?

Can I have two? Procrastinate. Spent time alone without my children.

What is your greatest achievement?

Dad to two amazing little but now big people . Thrown it all in and went to study for a Fine Art Degree. My first solo show was this year.

Tell me a secret about you:

I dated a TV personality and didn't know who she was till people kept stopping her to chat. I just thought she had a lot of friends. Found it hilarious, it didn't last long, it was all surface and no substance for me.

If you could go back in time to age 20 with your current life experience, what would you do differently?

I would be more forward and see the other side, telling myself there is a positive to everything. I'd make the most of my skills and the way I relate to people. I wouldn't be so scared or doubt myself. I would care less about what others said if it was a good thing that I was doing. I'd love more, I'd be more compassionate. I'd have shone and done the things my heart wanted to do much quicker.

There is a 15 year old standing in front of you. What life advice would you give him/her?

Always follow your heart, love more, forgive if you can then move on. But do not forget. You can only change yourself, you cannot change anyone but you. You can change the way you feel about something too.

Don't have expectancies but Carry your dreams with you. Just because someone says no, there'll be the right person who'll say yes.

If something is too good to be true, then it is. Treat everyday as a gift, like it was your last.

Treat fear as a friend to push you further, but not so as to come to any harm.

Treat others like you'd want to be treated. People may not know what it is, but they'll recognise humility...Oh yes, and try and do everything in moderation... except love thats the best.

When you are an elderly person, sitting in your rocking chair and you look back on your life, what do you want to have achieved?

That I'm able to to sit in a rocking chair and have seen my children grow up into amazing human beings!

Give me one word that sums up your life journey thus far: Ethereal

What is the meaning of life?

The meaning of life? I have nothing, but I have it all. I have love. Passing on a healthier planet you future generations.

'Large was his bounty, and his soul sincere, Heav'n did a recompense as largely send:

He gave to Mis'ry all he had, a tear, He gain'd from Heav'n ('twas all he wish'd) a friend.

Thomas Gray- 'Elegy written in a country churchyard'

Name: Soyoun Kim
Age: 36
Gender: Female
Country: South Korea
Occupation: Brand Manager

Do you believe in God?

Yes. I'm a christian from mother's womb. So I believe God from the time when I was born.

Belief is a natural thing for me.

What is the worst thing you've ever done?

Nothing?!? I believe it might be the utmost efforts of whatever I've done.

Yes. It's too much positive thinking! However, it makes me have more confidence by myself.

What is your greatest achievement?

To publish my own book. It was my one on my bucket list.

The category didn't matter, just whatever I'm interested in. I tried to write this from the age of 20.

Visual merchandising, Graffiti, Travel etc. Finally, I achieved this 2 years ago when I was 34. It's an essay and travel guide book about Dubai (UAE) where I spent time for 6 months.

Tell me a secret about you:

Um...

Secret is just secret

There are no secrets. I'm a very open-minded person with nothing to hide.

If you could go back in time to age 20 with your current life experience, what would you do differently?

To use my time wisely, efficiently. Study hard when I study, and play hard when I play.

I think I was an indecisive between study and play. If I could go back, I'd do better study/play/dating whatever.

There is a 15 year old standing in front of you. What life advice would you give him/her?

It's in the same answer with the above question."Study hard when I study, and play hard when I play."Youth is once and an irrevocable.

When you are an elderly person, sitting in your rocking chair and you look back on your life, what do you want to have achieved?

It's so sad a question just when I think about this. If I decline in physical strength, I'll look back upon my life with my loved ones. Just eat tasty food, talk about memories that we have.

Nothing to achieve; Enjoy the rest of life.

Give me one word that sums up your life journey thus far: Challenge!

My youth was the time of challenge. When I was 26, I liked to study abroad so I decided to go to the UK even though I couldn't speak English very well. It was my first challenge.

After that time, I've done many new challenges such as certificated musical, flower tea sommelier and to join a music band - a cappella group. Moreover, I tried my own business with my career. It was a fashion business and I did this for 3 years.

Also I applied for a business project supported by the Government and I got a chance to live in Dubai for 6months. (The essay which I've published was made from an experience in this time)

I think my life journey is 'challenge' from 20's until now.

What is the meaning of life?

It's quite a difficult question. Well, I think Life is journey. New chances in life, that I meet, are unfamiliar but also interesting.

Every year, every time, people meet new chances and choices. It makes them take their own way like a journey.

My life was a journey in a city break until middle of 30s and it's moving slowly to countryside.I feel more confident and relaxed with wide view. However, it will be a longer journey than the time I walked until now.

Name: R.O Murray – PPP (Pistol Packing Pastor)

Age: 70

Gender: Male

Country: Texas

Occupation: Cowboy Pastor and Motivational Speaker

Do you believe in God?

I have always known there was a God because of my parents taking me to Sunday School and church but I never had any dealing with Him or relationship with Him.

Sometime in the early 1970's I had a man witness to me rather convincingly about God. I pondered some of the things he said for a couple of days and then those thoughts fell by the wayside. As I look back, the Lord was trying to get my attention. However, I went about my business without realising that He was calling me.

As I was out on the town one night drinking, fighting, and tearing up a couple of bars, God roped me, dallied up hard and fast and let me run the slack out of my rope. Later on that night I ran out of hope - Oh, the pain, suffering and agony as I was put uncomfortably jail.

A long story short: I was in isolation with no one anywhere close to me. Then I heard an audible voice saying, "It's now or never." in a firm, no-nonsense tone. I looked around without finding anyone then it dawned on me that it was God speaking to me. I said, "Later," and shrugged it off.

Perhaps some 30 minutes later I heard that voice again. "It's now or never!" in a firm, no-nonsense tone again. As I started to think about what I'd heard, my blood suddenly ran cold. All at once I could feel that cold traversing through my body from the inside out. I knew right then that there would not be another chance to accept the Lord and my future would be extremely bleak if I didn't.

Me being a cowboy, trading cattle and horses, it is my nature to try and swing a deal, so I tried swinging a deal with God as I knew I was in a bad fix. There was no way I was getting out of jail because of the hold and the charges the police put on me. But God would not deal, plain and simple. No trades. I asked Jesus into my heart right there in that jail cell and an unexplainable peace fell upon me. I promptly went to sleep without any worries.

5 or 6 hours later a jailer called my name and said to me, "There is no way this should happen but you are free to go."

A year after all of my court dates I had a district judge check my criminal record. He reported that I had no criminal record of any kind - the slate was wiped clean and even my poaching deer convictions had disappeared.

So, do I believe in God? Absolutely positively YES.

What is the worst thing you've ever done?

This isn't a fair question trying to pick the worst of the worse things I have done. The worst things are the things that had lasting effects on others and the emotional pain I caused whether intentional or unintentional. The physical pain I have caused does not compare with the emotional pain and suffering that I have caused others throughout my life. One usually heals from the physical harm but the emotional pain and distress is always long lasting and seldom forgotten. Words really can hurt worse than sticks and stones.

What is your greatest achievement?

There are several great achievements that I have accomplished and some that I am still achieving.

My greatest achievement will last me for all eternity and that is I am becoming the person that God wants me to be. This is a lifetime work in progress. I am not where I want to be but I am no longer where I once was. As I work on my greatest achievement I can help others reach their goals and change their lives for the better.

Tell me a secret about you:

First, if I tell you, it won't be a secret any longer.

That being said, I am a sceptic and private person as I have been hurt so many times by people whom I have trusted and have built up walls around me.

This is kind of an oxymoron since I am an optimist, but it is so true. But, being in the public and dealing with the public day in and day out, I can be misunderstood, misquoted and misinterpreted for the slightest thing. It seems that those closest to me hurt and/or betray me the most. Often with those I don't really know, it doesn't bother me so much. To hear the rumors, back stabbing, etc. from the 'outsiders' that I don't really know doesn't bother me because I don't have a relationship with them.

Now I'm back to the emotional pain. Words hurt more than sticks and stones.

Consequently, I am often defensive when I don't need to be. My voice and body language often reveal this defensiveness. I don't laugh enough and I am too serious and intense the majority of the time.

If you could go back in time to age 20 with your current life experience, what would you do differently?

I would have established a relationship with the Lord first and foremost. There is so much to this relationship that would have saved me tons of pain, heartache and money.

I would have learned to love and applied that love to everyone - even the unlovable.

I would have laughed more and been much less intense.

I would have established a financial plan for my life all the way to the end with leaving an inheritance to my loved ones.

I would have sought out mentors to advise and guide me through life's ups and downs. Several older mentors would have made a world of difference to me for 50 years.

I would have investigated the many things that I was involved in/with more thoroughly and sought more advice. (Back then there was no internet, computers, cell-phones etc)

I would have dismissed the "Naysayers" and not played the "What If" game.

I would have been more of an adventurist and more inquisitive.

I would have implemented my answers to the question below.

There is a 15 year old standing in front of you. What life advice would you give him/her?

The first thing I would say is to have a relationship with God.

The second thing - Be your own person and be true to who you are and where you are going. Learn to laugh and laugh at yourself. Laughter is the best medicine for your life.

Thirdly, don't listen to all the negatives that will come your way. Too many people will not want you to achieve your goals and become happy with your life because they aren't happy with theirs.

The next thing would be to set goals: Long range goals, intermediate goals and short term goals. This really is a vision statement. Review the goals/vision statement at least a couple of times a year as things are changing constantly. Establish how to obtain your goals. How are you going to accomplish them?

Be an optimistic realist. Seek the Lord's wisdom. Evaluate but don't be hasty. Obtain knowledge.

Remember that life owes you nothing and you owe life your best efforts.

Leave people much better than you found them.

Oh, and learn to love! Love yourself as well.

When you are an elderly person, sitting in your rocking chair and you look back on your life, what do you want to have achieved?

I am considered elderly at my age, however, I am not sitting in a rocking chair and have no plans to do so. I have things to do and people to help, bless and love.

I hope to leave this little part of the world that I am in a better place because of me being here.

I desire to touch hearts and change lives through my experience, wisdom, knowledge, and love and to encourage people not to be so serious and to laugh a lot.

The statistics reveal that no one gets out alive - We all will die.

The Lord has blessed me by having me go to different parts of the world and different cultures, from the jungles of Central America to Australia to Romania, The Mayan descendants in Mexico and not least of all, the rural beauty of south -east Texas. And I am not done. I am still an adventurer that is curious and wanting to see more of what is out there.

I want people to know that I cared for them and I did my best to bless and help them.

Give me one word that sums up your life journey thus far: Exciting

What is the meaning of life?

Life is to be lived to its fullest as this is our training for the eternal life to come — either good or bad.

Good meaning that heaven is the end destiny because of your relationship with Jesus as your Lord and Savior — the only way to heaven.

Bad meaning you don't have to do anything for hell to be the final destiny for all eternity.

There are no do-overs once you are dead — make your decision now while you still can.

Here's an extra:

A real man is the kind of man that when his feet hit the floor each morning, the devil says, "Oh crud, he's up!"

Folks, life is too short to wake up with regrets so love the people who treat you right and forgive the one's who don't just because you can.

Believe that everything happens for a reason. If you get a second chance, grab it with both hands. If it changes your life, let it.

Take a few minutes to think before you act when you're mad. Forgive quickly. God never said life would be easy. He just promised it would be worth it.

Name: Stefanie Smith

Age: 48

Gender: Female

Country: England

Occupation: Medically retired nurse

Do you believe in God?

I am a Pagan, I believe in a God and Goddess, the co-dependency of male and female energies.

What is the worst thing you've ever done?

Difficult one this - I think I'd have to say committing adultery, although my (now ex) husband was a narcissist and had driven me right down to breaking point with a massive lack of self belief - so when a male colleague showed me interest and support I was drawn in.

What is your greatest achievement?

Motherhood.

Tell me a secret about you:

I am a survivor of childhood sexual abuse.

If you could go back in time to age 20 with your current life experience, what would you do differently?

I wouldn't have married the man I did - I believed no-one else would have me - I wish I could have believed more in myself. The only drawback with that is that I wouldn't have had my children.

There is a 15 year old standing in front of you. What life advice would you give him/her?

Believe in and love yourself. Happiness is more important than money.

When you are an elderly person, sitting in your rocking chair and you look back on your life, what do you want to have achieved?

I always said I want to look back and be happy with the choices I made - even if they turned out to be the wrong ones - I am a firm believer that it's the chances we don't take that we regret. My number one bucket list item is to go to Machu Picchu - and I will get there!!

Give me one word that sums up your life journey thus far: Experimental!

What is the meaning of life?

Love and happiness.

Name: Randy C. Blue

Age: 48 on the outside

Gender: Male

Country: The Netherlands (for now)

Occupation: College Professor

Do you believe in God?

No, I don't, but that does that stop me from hoping God believes in me. I'm human that way; always hoping to be special. Did you know that only 7% of the world's population suffers from an absence of belief in a deity? Well, it is my belief that the majority is often wrong. Why does there have to be a God? Because we want there to be one? WE want a lot. It's in our nature. One life won't do. We want an afterlife, and it had better be good. Think eternal bliss (not 80 years, no, no, no) and streets paved of gold (naturally).

I once told my friends I had heard God speak to me, but no one believed me. Even the local minister didn't believe me. How ironic is that? Think about it: Believe in God, boys and girls. Just don't tell anyone you had lunch with him the other day because that would mean you're delusional.

What is the worst thing you've ever done?

Made a cat fly. Luckily it landed on its feet. (Of course it wasn't my own cat!)

What is your greatest achievement?

I wish I could say I built the pyramids, but at the same time such a wish would only illustrate my point - that we are a narcissistic bunch. I think we should embrace it as a laudable quality and feel better about ourselves. So, yes, I built the pyramids. I also created a home for my wife and Bollywood Princess (they are the same person), my furry feline friends Mongo the Fat Cat and his annoying little sister, Pebbles the wannabe opera singer who refuses to zip it when she's in the middle of a concerto de meowo at 4 o'clock in the morning. Even my neighbor's cocky rooster is considering suicide.

Tell me a secret about you:

Nobody knows who I am. All I can say right now is this: I'm not Batman, but don't tell anyone or they'll know it, too. But, seriously, nobody knows who I am. That's dark, eh?

If you could go back in time to age 20 with your current life experience, what would you do differently?

I would make all new mistakes and have the necessary experience to put each one into perspective. I would also remind myself to buy silver and gold instead of depositing my money into a bank account that thrives on inflation and zero interest.

There is a 15 year old standing in front of you. What life advice would you give him/her?

Well, as long as we're not talking unsolicited advice, here is my top five. *Number one: Life is too short to have a career fetish*. What I mean by that is that friends and loved-ones might be more important than connections, connections, connections and the-universe-that-is-me.

Number two: Don't waste your life capturing every moment of it with your smart phone. Put it away and look at what is in front of you. Make it a visceral experience, not a virtual experience. Try to remember it in all its glory (especially if it involves nasty teenager nudie stuff). Don't depend on your phone to remember it *for* you. You are not one of those pathetic, feeble humans in *WALL-E*. Think, walk, remember.

Number three: Don't trust anyone who says, "I have an important appointment at 10." There is no such thing.

Number four: Money makes you happy. People who say it doesn't are either poor, unimaginative or both. Money opens doors. Don't virtue-signal by branding it the devil. All you need is a good heart and you will open all the right ones.

Number five: You were not born to be anybody's puppet, so don't study law because that is what is expected of you, don't get married because that is what is expected of you, and don't have children because that is what is expected of you. In fact, question everything that people, parents and pundits in particular present as truth or virtue. There is always an agenda. (Yes, that includes religion. I'm using the R-word here.) Because you see, dear fifteen-year-old, parents want you to accept, nay, embrace their set of beliefs, no questions asked, and to be like them. Why? Well, for you to go through the same motions makes for the perfect quick fix. It's a much craved bar of chocolate called confirmation because, unfortunately, sooner or later you will find (if you haven't already) that grownups know diddly-squat about life, so they've made it their business to hide their insecurities and to appear knowing. They are like Santa Clause that way. In short, they want you to accept their set of beliefs as canon because they love MINI-MEs. (Our narcissistic predisposition is a force to be reckoned with, young Padawan.) Even when they urge you to go and find your own, unique path in life, what they secretly want is for you to get good grades, find a good job, find a good husband or wife, make a kid or two (good or bad, preferably good but we *need* a grandchild), and basically do what their own parents wanted them to do and believe, so... now... it's... your... turn. Let's give this phenomenon a serious name and call it the circle of life. Don't be too harsh on them, though, because self-love and love are sometimes very hard to distinguish. They want "what's best for you." Incidentally, what is best for you is what is best for them, too. Just saying.

Number six in my top five: Eggshell walking is not cool, so screw all SJWs and PC fetishists. Pardon my Swedish.

When you are an elderly person, sitting in your rocking chair and you look back on your life, what do you want to have achieved?

Putting a gun to my head, I would say that I will want to have achieved that my wife's decision to spend her life with me way back then was a good one for her in spite of my darker shade of blue and my rapidly declining good looks.

Give me one word that sums up your life journey thus far: Erraticallicious

What is the meaning of life?

There is no such thing. Seeking meaning in everything is a human need. It's our special brand of tunnel vision. Whatever we feel, do or don't, our biology dictates that we experience life a certain, limited way: that we see it through human spectacles. Yet we insist that our interpretations; not those of our cats, of course, the ants in my picnic basket or the pigeons terrorizing the neighborhood (what do they know?) are canon or, worse, truth. If you happen to think you are delicious, you can blame the ingredients used to create the mouth-watering dish you are to explain why you want life to have meaning. For one, we are biologically equipped to be thinkers. To add insult to injury, we are bipolar thinkers who like to put everything and everyone in bipolar Walt Disney boxes. Let the ticking commence: *Good or bad? Right or wrong? Day or night? Happy or sad?* Add to this mix our human self-awareness, our human self-importance ("Rulers of the world!" "We aren't part of nature! We protect it!" "It's a sign from God!"), and our ability to fantasize, fantasize and, yes, fantasize, and what you've got makes perfect sense.

What it all boils down to is we *want* our existence to have meaning. Our benevolent narcissism dictates that we can't be here for no reason: *Surely, I'm here for a reason. Hello, just look at me! Hello? Hello?* (No wonder we invented the iPhone.) But things don't have to have meaning. The world can be beautiful, enjoyable and awful (see, I'm bipolar as well) without us imposing this biological need for things to mean something in relation to... no surprise there... us. The way I see it, life has no meaning. We exist and that's about it. So, ironically, it is up to us to give life meaning. Now, does that mean we can't enjoy life? Speaking as a privileged narcissistic western male, I'd say, No, it doesn't. Do enjoy it. Enjoy it to the full. Try that juicy melon called life. Take a big bite and let the juices flow, baby! Just don't be a puppet. Listen to Mr. Keaton. He might have something interesting to say to you. *Oh Captain, my Captain!*

Please take everything I've said with a grain of salt. Add some pepper. Maybe some basil. Chew it a couple of times and ask yourself if you are willing to swallow it hook, line and sinker. My advice is to first read everything else that's on the menu and then order the dish that you find appealing. If you don't like what you have ordered, tell the waiter to return it to the kitchen and ask the cook to try again or maybe prep you something else. You're not destined to eat meat or not eat meat, you know? Pig, shark or chicken. Life is about choices.

Name: Su Bramley

Age: 44

Gender: Female

Country: England

Occupation: Company director/ Accountant

Do you believe in God?

I believe in a deity that is the hub of the universe. I believe many deities come from the master deity.

What is the worst thing you've ever done?

When I was a child aged about 8 I was goaded by other children much older than me to physically hurt another child. I smacked her head against the park railings, just once, but once is too many times. That memory sticks with me forever and makes me feel physically sick.

What is your greatest achievement?

I could say my career or becoming a mum, but truly it is being comfortable in my own skin.

Tell me a secret about you:

I don't have any secrets, I'm very transparent; an open book. What people don't know about me isn't worth knowing.

If you could go back in time to age 20 with your current life experience, what would you do differently?

Nothing - it's made me who I am today.

There is a 15 year old standing in front of you. What life advice would you give him/her?

You're not from Stepford, you're very different to other people, so stop trying to be!

When you are an elderly person, sitting in your rocking chair and you look back on your life, what do you want to have achieved?

To have enjoyed but left the rat race; to be in the countryside with the stars and the knowledge that I ran a successful business - a successful family, and a successful marriage.

Give me one word that sums up your life journey thus far: CRAAAAAAZY!

What is the meaning of life?

We walk the earth to grow spiritually..to learn from ourselves and from others, however, the answer lies within. Once we master that, we become comfortable in our own skin and no one can offend.

Never a judge a person until you have walked 2 moons in his shoes.

Fear is an irrational emotion - forget everything and run or face everything and rise.

Fail - first attempt in learning.

If life was easy everyone would live it forever.

Don't aspire to be the next anybody, aspire to be the first YOU!

Be honest - be open - be transparent.

Be comfortable in your own skin then no one or nothing can offend.

Love lots - laugh lots - cry often.

It's OK to feel shitty but don't dwell. When there is shit in the pot, flush it away.

And, if all else fails, put it in the fook it bucket and move on!

Name: Rick Guidotti

Age: 68

Gender: Male

Country: USA

Occupation: Guitarist for The Turtles for 30 years...now retired.

Do you believe in God?

Oh....you want me to write the whole book for you eh??? The short answer is yes & no...MY gods...not YOUR God!

I went to Catholic grade school and had their propaganda forced on my through childhood. Forgot about it in public high school. Then, had 2 years of Catholic College where Religion was a required course and I was dreading it. But it turned out I had a GREAT priest professor who taught us about ALL religions and really opened my mind and broadened my paradigms. I learned about Buddhism and the Hindus and really liked Zen. I have also been interested in Science my whole life and highly educated myself on everything from Astronomy to Quantum Physics. I've also been interested in Metaphysics but not completely buying into all the *woowoo*. I've come to my own conclusions: There is no God up there who wants anything. No one to answer your prayers - no *chosen people* You don't have to wear black, grow a beard, go to church, kill the infidels, not eat pork, or accept Jesus Christ. In fact, I'm amazed that people still buy into that extortion plot claiming a human sacrifice was needed to save humanity from their original sins. Really? And those who think The Bible is The Word Of God - did you stone your daughter to death when you learned she had committed adultery? Well, you didn't follow His Word did you? How about "Thou shall not kill"? Why do we have a military? And there is the old question about evil. Did God create THAT? Does He ALLOW that? Is He powerless over that?

All this nonsense (and mass murder) because we SO want to humanize God. "We are made in his image"... so...we made him like us...an egotistical asshole! Have I offended everybody yet? I'm not finished! When you study physics, you learn that there are no such things as *things*. At the smallest level, tiny fields of energy are vibrating in and out of existence. Consciousness makes them decide to *be* somewhere at a moment in Time. These tiny energy fields organize themselves into atoms, molecules, germs, plants, bugs & people. Sure looks like *things* to us! But it is really only energy fields. Energy that is constantly creating. Every snowflake ever fallen through history, a unique creation. Every dawn and sunset...365 time a year...for 4 1/2 billion years... UNIQUE! Every blade of grass, little worm, cloud in the sky. Every human, an individual creation that sees the world from its own personal viewpoint. So, where is God? Who said there is only one? And why did we believe them? The Egyptians were right, our Sun IS a God. It created Earth and gives it Life. No question about that! But wait, then every star must also be a God! What about a galaxy? A BIG God? Yep! Big Gods...Little Gods... EVERYWHERE! Can't we lump them all together into One True God? NOPE! You're trying to humanize Him again. It's easier to try & love ONE thing than than to to try to love EVERYTHING. But remember, there are no things! Confused yet? God is the creative force of energy. It is both miraculous and awful. But it only seems awful when we judge it by our human wishes. Everything is Divine. Everything is God. Treat everything with the respect you would give your God! So, wonder at the beauty of an old oak tree...the miracle of a flower...the life in a drop of pond water...even the dog shit on the sidewalk - it's God in action! And don't get me started on Hell! Any God who will burn you forever because of something you did or didn't do is an asshole! My Gods' don't care what you do, but YOU should care. If YOU care, God cares! Yes.YOU are God. Maybe not ALL powerful but FAR more powerful than you can imagine!

What is the worst thing you've ever done?

There may be things I have repressed & can't recall. It also depends on whose standards you chose.

I killed 5 fetuses...had to...it was either them or me. If I hadn't, I'd be married to a lesbian, a bunch of boring fat gals, or raising some gay guy's kid.

What is your greatest achievement?

Fucking Peggy the waitress? How 'bout when me & my gal did it on a volcano? Seeing 2 total solar eclipses? Hiking glaciers in Alaska?

Actually, it was starting my band Rave Up. In the early 80's we were SO popular that Beatle George Harrison heard about us...decided to come in for a listen...liked us... stayed all night...shook my hand saying,"You do a good John!" We were playing Beatle tunes for him and this was one year after Lennon's death. What a compliment! From that band I went on to be the guitarist for Flo & Eddie of The Turtles and worked with them for 30 years!

Tell me a secret about you:

If I had one, would I put it in a book for all to read? My biggest secrets were hiding the 2 illegal abortions which nearly killed my girlfriend from both of our Catholic parents. My gal went on to become a lesbian - was I to blame? She says no, but still, I wonder. Thinking deeper, I suppose I have hidden from everybody the fact that I am borderline paranoid. I've always lived with a lot of self imposed fear. I was afraid to be outgoing, to talk to new people, afraid to phone people thinking I would be bothering them. Afraid to take the advice of my parents. Afraid I made the wrong choice of a girlfriend....the wrong choices in Life. Funny thing is, put a guitar in my hand and I can be the life of the party. Take it away, I'm a wallflower!

If you could go back in time to age 20 with your current life experience, what would you do differently?

There is a lot, I'm afraid. Can we go back further? By age 20 I had already made plenty of wrong decisions!

Somehow, as a young child, I decided (probably from watching TV & movies) that the cool guys were quiet & shy. And so I sat back & watched while the guys who WEREN'T quiet & shy got all the gals & good jobs. I didn't want to talk to old people. I learned late in life that old people have the BEST stories and advice! If I had followed the advice of my parents...I would have made new friends who could have helped my career...wouldn't have wasted thousands of dollars on cigarettes. But I was a rebel. I would have been less afraid, less self conscious, made friends and stayed in touch with them. Said *yes* to adventure instead of *no* out of fear of the unknown. Can we stop here before I get depressed??? One last thing: when working a job I despised...I should have QUIT! Instead, I thought the honorable thing to do was tough it out & stay the course (of misery). Translate into 8 years of self imposed HELL!

There is a 15 year old standing in front of you. What life advice would you give him/her?

Always use/insist on condoms! One in four people have Herpes - you have it for life - you DON'T want it! You also don't want some gal you shacked up with after a night of drinking to become knocked up. This will ruin your life, her life and the life of the child. Just thinking about *getting inside* will put sperm on the tip of Mr. Johnson... you don't need an orgasm to get her pregnant. And don't become a drug, alcohol or cigarette addict. It will waste your money and your life. Never be afraid to chat with a beauty who seems *out of your league*. (But what will I say?) Ask her about HER life, and listen closely. People LOVE to talk about themselves. If you listen, they will like you! If you brag about YOUR life & try to impress them, they won't like you. f you fail to *score*...no big deal! It wasn't meant to be - move on and don't take it personally. There are PLENTY of fish in the sea. But if you are afraid to even try, you get a guaranteed LOSE! Then you'll beat yourself up thinking what a chickenshit you are!

When you are an elderly person, sitting in your rocking chair and you look back on your life, what do you want to have achieved?

Hmmm, I already AM an old person in my rocker thinking back (thanks Jules!)...and I think too much emphasis is put on the word *achievement*.

By who's standards? Did I get rich? No, but I spent a large portion of my life getting paid to do what I loved (play music). Did I get famous? Only locally. But I was highly respected in my field by friends, fans & peers. Did I get married, buy a house & raise a family? Nope....but is that an achievement? Everybody does that! Most of my friends did...and then they died. Why them & not me? One thing I know: I entertained a LOT of people & made them happy - if only for a few hours. I tried to leave the world a better place than how I found it and succeeded in my own little ways. Hey, I am no longer afraid to talk to pretty women! Except now I'm to old for then to even consider.

RATS! And these days? I'm STILL famous (only in my neighborhood) as *The Telescope Guy*.

In the summer I set up my telescope on my busy sidewalk in Hollywood and show the moon & planets to pedestrians. Just the other night a pretty gal told me that I make our street special & nice! I tell people they are not separate but actually part of the stars they are looking at. Many have been moved to tears and say that is something they really needed to hear! One guy said hanging out with me was the best night of his life! Not bad eh? And the beat goes on...

Give me one word that sums up your life journey thus far: COOL!

What is the meaning of life?

Here is a murky hole of quicksand I'd like to hop over as there are many ways to answer.

Each of us is The Universe looking at Itself from a unique point of view. Each person will have their own answer.

It's easy to fall into the traps of Karma, Reincarnation, learning Life Lessons...

I'm not sayin' it ain't so - but I'm skipping that stuff.

Take away the Religion, Philosophy, Spirituality, etc, and what have we got?

Our galaxy made stars, some of them blew up. They didn't really *die* - they sent heavy elements out into Space. It was a creative process. Out of this heavier material, our sun was born. Earth was also born with the left over heavy stuff. And germs & fish & trees & flowers and animals & Man all naturally popped out of the ground. (Unless we were seeded by Aliens)

And we were given eyes to look at the mountains, the clouds in the sky, the moon & stars, the ocean and go "WOW!"

But then, we are blind the destruction we are causing our world.

We were given ears to listen to the birds and talk to each other and create beautiful music & go "WOW!".

But when politicians speak, we only hear what we want to hear.

The Universe gave us Taste to enjoy food, then we eat too much and make ourselves sick.

We have noses to smell the roses but delight in our farts.

Ahhh....the soothing touch from a loved one.

While on the other side of the planet someone is tortured for lack of a religious belief.

Why are we here? To experience all this and more. The Universe constantly creates new experiences.

But never feel like you are trapped, stuck on this *Ride*. You operate it!

You ARE The Universe. How big is a piece of Infinity? Answer: Infinite!

All the power of the stars & galaxies are yours and mine! We are Gods who have forgotten their power! We are co-creating our Reality together! Be careful what you say & do!

YOU give Life meaning by observing it and acting upon it.

When I hear people say, "Praise the Lord!", they almost have it right.

Unfortunately many of them think they are worshiping some bearded guy in the sky who is easily pissed off. But if you step outside and enjoy the fresh air - sniff the flowers - watch the bees - listen to the birds - marvel at the clouds - enjoy the shade of a tree...the warmth of the sun, or even the wetness of the rain or the stinging of the cold; if you experience it fully and appreciate it, you ARE worshiping God! We are The Universe enjoying itself in all its discoveries.Don't get in the way of that!

I got your *meaning* right HERE!

I've come to the conclusion everything is alive. Our definition of Life is far too narrow. We think things have to eat, poop & make babies to be alive. I say, that is wrong.

EVERYTHING is conscious! Atoms feel & have memories. This explains a lot. A true Psychic can pick up an object and give information about the owner because they can feel the memories of the atoms. A place can be haunted... not because a soul is lost or trapped, but because the atoms in the wall retain and can play back the emotions they recall. Emotions exist in their own field of reality. Remember, EVERYTHING is an energy field.

Thoughts and emotions are as real as the *physical* things around us. Be careful what you think!

I feel if you love something, ANYTHING -somehow, at some level - IT KNOWS! And I feel it loves you back!

I believe the stars are conscious beings. Galaxies have personalities. And one of our most precious gifts is our limitless imagination!

Every car, building, phone, TV, internet blah -blah -blah, started out as an idea in someone's head. We are surrounded by our ideas! Some good, some perhaps not so good. I may not believe in a Heaven where I sit in the glory of God the Father. However, in my imagination I DO create a better world where everyone is nice: no wars or military, no police, no crime, animals that don't need to eat each other, plenty of beautiful friendly women, hehe etc....

I hope that if I *move on*, I go THERE!

Which brings us to the question of *The Afterlife*.

Two choices here: either there is or there isn't.

If there isn't, then all this is bullshit & who cares & fuck you & everyone in your family and this was all for nothing. GAME OVER MAN!

I don't believe that. Science tells us that energy can not be created or destroyed. And I am energy = immortality!

I like to make the analogy of an ant. The ants outside my place know my steps and the crack in the sidewalk and where to forage for food. All they need to know. They don't know of Western Ave (blocks away) - San Diego (90 miles) - the ocean -Jupiter - the Andromeda Galaxy. But yet we think we are SO smart. Why, WE can see billions of light years away!!! Guess what? We are way, way, WAY smaller than that ant, and probably know LESS! There is light SO far away that it will NEVER reach our eyes! The part of our HUGE Universe that we see MUST be a TINY fraction of what is out there. And I'm suppose to figure out what is going on? I'm clueless! And so I chose to believe in bug eyed aliens that can travel faster that the speed of light, walk through walls and alter our DNA on a whim. Time & Space are illusions we create to give the dream of *living a life*. Enjoy The Ride. We came here to experience it ALL. The Joy & Sorrow - Pleasure & Pain - Gain & Loss - Love & Loneliness. A journey from the Depths to the Heights. Or sometimes, the other way! Often going down dead end roads sidetracked into an alley; blazing a new path or following the Yellow Brick Road! Slowly trying to comprehend an Infinity of Constant Creation. Just be aware of the miracles around you & say, "WOW, what a trip!"

Name: Sue

Age: 54

Gender: Female

Country: England

Occupation: Insurance

Do you believe in God?

I don't believe in a god that is external to oneself, however, I believe that everyone has a divine element of their own - effectively, an internal higher being.

I believe that the many named gods and goddesses that are "known" or described are simply icons which epitomise specific sets of characteristics and which we may use to invoke the relevant powers within ourselves.

What is the worst thing you've ever done?

Married, or rather had cause to divorce a person with NPD / PDA. However, despite how awful the whole experience was, it did lead to me learning an awful lot about myself. Without that experience, I probably wouldn't be the person I am today

What is your greatest achievement?

I'm not sure there is one – there are several equally valuable things but for different reasons.

In a personal sense, learning to find and express the authentic me. Sounds like a bit of a cliche but it is necessary to discover a whole lot about yourself that isn't very useful, and is frankly quite scary, before you can dare ,or feel free, to be real. Also having long standing friends who know all of this.

In a practical sense, remaining as financially independent as possible. This has been a very important factor in being able to escape unhappy or unhealthy situations. Also, achieving a degree via OU whilst working full time and in a very difficult marriage.

Arriving here and now still reasonably sane, wanting to carry on learning, enjoying a variety of activities and still having a sense of humour.

Tell me a secret about you:

I could not have children.; this is not, however, a regret in any way as there are dogs, and I have mothered step children.:)

If you could go back in time to age 20 with your current life experience, what would you do differently?

I would apply the knowledge I have about relationships, and myself so that I would not engage in unhappy unions or endure unhealthy workplaces for far too long. I would also make an effort to retain the fitness that I had then rather than becoming lazy with my body and arriving at the round me I am today. I would seize every opportunity to travel and learn. I would not let things encumber me.

There is a 15 year old standing in front of you. What life advice would you give him/her?

Respect yourself & others. Take the time to learn what this means. Apart from that, not a lot, as a teenager needs to follow his / her own path, make his /her own mistakes and learn just as I did. Probably better to be a good role model than to preach or advise.

When you are an elderly person, sitting in your rocking chair and you look back on your life, what do you want to have achieved?

To feel satisfied and grateful for the life I have lived. A reasonable amount of happiness. To have enough to meet my needs.

Give me one word that sums up your life journey thus far: Eclectic

What is the meaning of life?

Life is its own meaning.

The road may be long or short, no one knows where it leads, there may be monsters or pretty gardens on the way, and all will teach us what we need to know.

Name: Arthur's Lad

Age: 60

Gender: Male

Country: UK

Occupation: Geologist

Do you believe in God?

Yes, but not in the sense of a great Creator figure floating around in the heavens like some Renaissance work of art. For me God is the result of man's need for a deity who makes salvation possible. This need has probably developed and strengthened since the days of the earliest humans.

What is the worst thing you've ever done?

First marriage! Bit of an error but came out it relatively unscathed.

What is your greatest achievement?

Having children, 2 great boys, wouldn't be without them for the world.

Tell me a secret about you:

Generally, I'm not a bit superstitious apart from 'the number of the devil'. I'm not going to write it. I don't even like '66' never mind the full thing. I hate seeing personalised number plates with those numbers on.

If you could go back in time to age 20 with your current life experience, what would you do differently?

Mainly work related stuff. I would consider myself and family first more often and maybe be less afraid of the consequences of certain actions in the workplace. I would have left one particular position long before I eventually did. On a personal basis I'd make more of opportunities that arose than I did, because generally they never come again.

There is a 15 year old standing in front of you. What life advice would you give him/her?

Always remember life isn't a rehearsal, you are only here once, make the most of every opportunity that comes your way.

Don't work too hard, put yourself first, do things that make you happy, work to live, not the other way around. If you are unhappy there is usually a better option available, maybe right under your nose. Make the most of time spent with your parents, try to understand them, they won't always be around. Travel, but not necessarily to the other side of the world, see as much as you can of the area or country you live in.

When you are an elderly person, sitting in your rocking chair and you look back on your life, what do you want to have achieved?

Looked after my parents. Raised a family of my own who are happy and successful, ensured they had a decent education and given them some financial security. Discovered my personal history roots and passed this information on.

Give me one word that sums up your life journey thus far: Easy

What is the meaning of life?

Being a part of the whole world around you, trying to see and understand all you can. Have a purpose but go with the flow, don't fight against it.

Name: Sue

Age: 51

Gender: Female

Country: UK

Occupation: Hairdresser and mother

Do you believe in God?

I don't think I do but when it suits me & in times of desperation I pray I'm wrong and have been known to ask for help and a miracle from who, if anyone, is up there.

I believe that there is no destiny, Karma or fate, we are the only ones in control of our lives

What is the worst thing you've ever done?

The worst thing I've ever done in whose eyes ?

I'm sure lots of people I've known could give lots of different answers to this one.

I'm finding it really hard to pick an answer to this: I've lied to friends, I've cheated on loved ones , I've judged when I had no right, so I'm going with the answer of the worst thing I've done is not always be true to myself & what I wanted in life.

What is your greatest achievement?

My greatest achievement is obviously my children , I look at them in sheer amazement that I have managed to raise such balanced happy beings. How the hell did I not fuck that job up I will never know.

Tell me a secret about you:

My secret is I stole a crisp £5 note from my friend Karen when we were 13. Karen had received the birthday money from an Aunt in the post and had a moan that it wasn't a gift as such, i was annoyed how ungrateful she was & I was so jealous , I had never had that much money to my self so while Karen was down stairs having her tea leaving me alone in her room I took it from her window sill jewellery box and stuffed it in my pocket.

Four days later it was discovered missing and I was asked if I knew where it was , I totally denied all knowledge of it and our other friend Jayne got the blame and she was never welcomed in Karen's house again. I still to this day feel guilty for not only stealing but also lying & letting a friendship break up between Karen & Jayne and not ever being brave enough to own up that it was me .

With my stolen money I bought "everybody wants to rule the world" by Tears for Fears , a black eye liner and heaps of sweets; these items didn't ease my guilt and 38 yrs later I still feel the shame but cannot ever confess that it was me

If you could go back in time to age 20 with your current life experience, what would you do differently?

I would do so many things differently but the main thing would be to plan . Plan out how & when I want things to happen not to just go along with the flow of chance.

There is a 15 year old standing in front of you. What life advice would you give him/her?

There is a whole huge world out there , travel until you find where & what you want to be ... and don't smoke!

When you are an elderly person, sitting in your rocking chair and you look back on your life, what do you want to have achieved?

I'd like to think I will have achieved a sense of fulfilment just through seeing my children & grandchildren happy & feeling loved

Give me one word that sums up your life journey thus far: Content

What is the meaning of life?

The meaning of life is so so different for each & everyone of us, I think it lays in so many different words and meanings but the one word I world use is ACHIEVEMENT.

We are all striving to achieve our own goals, from a tiny otter building a damn to an aspiring architect building a city, from the country bumpkin wife building a cosy home to the Mafia building a cartel. We are all driven by some sort of achievement.

Name: Roger

Age: 70

Gender: Male

Country: USA

Occupation: Self-employed professional

Do you believe in God?

Yes.

What is the worst thing you've ever done?

Allowed my arrogance to get in the way of loving others and prevent me from treating them respectfully. I was raised as an only child until age eight by well-meaning but atheist liberal intellectual parents who followed the

Benjamin Spock / Fred Rogers hands-off "your kid is special" approach. As a result I was not truly humbled and disciplined until I learned to follow Christ.

What is your greatest achievement?

I married the woman who is my best friend, and we've shared that friendship and trust for the past 42 years.

Tell me a secret about you:

Don't really have any. By most folks' standards, I am pretty boring. I never murdered anyone, nor assumed a false identity to engage in wire fraud. I did support JFK back in the day, but in those days there were true liberals in the Democrat Party, not the red-eyed and black-hearted lunatics that control it today.

If you could go back in time to age 20 with your current life experience, what would you do differently?

Recognize and respond to the signs that were telling me, many years ago, that God had conferred His grace on me. I always knew He was there, from the beauty of general revelation, and the power that reached me through the music of the great, God-inspired composers. But I denied His invitation for many years, pursuing "self-actualization" and material goals. Everything about my life, from my marriage to my internal peace, has now been placed on an unshakeable foundation by God's grace, and my faith in Him and His son Jesus Christ. When I realized that, like Robert Crumb's "Mister Natural", I am just passin' thru this physical life, the daily worries about security and health, as well as my natural combativeness, all went away: Truly so.

There is a 15-year old standing in front of you. What life advice would you give him/her?

Disregard the communists, the "prosperity gospel" frauds, the "life coaches" who preach self-salvation and claim to pave your road to a utopia on earth. None of us can save ourselves from the total depravity that defines the fallen human condition. Only God's grace and faith in Jesus Christ can set you free. You'll discover the moral strength to stand firm against the waves of sexual filth that will try to wash you away. You'll realize that actions, and words, have consequences, and will choose yours more reasonably. You'll learn that love does conquer hate: If God is for you, who can stand against you?

When you are an elderly person sitting in your rocking chair, and you look back on your life, what do you want to have achieved?

A half-century of loving my wife as half of my own soul. And should I go first, leaving an earthly estate sufficient to keep her from worry. Some of us (who are better educated in apologetics) are called to be defenders of the faith. Others, like me, are called to be defenders of the faithFUL. I want to support persecuted Christians with resources. I want to defeat progressives and other advocates of over arching government with well-crafted words.

Give me one word that sums up your life journey so far: Blessed!

What is the meaning of life?

I see no "meaning" per se, only PURPOSE. And that purpose is to glorify God with one's behavior, one's attitudes, one's kindness, and one's thankful faith.

Name: Sue Tostevin

Age: 56

Gender: Female

Country: UK

Occupation: Business owner

Do you believe in God?

Absolutely.

What is the worst thing you've ever done?

Lied to my boss. Nothing major. His sister worked in the same company and asked me to provide her with a reference as she hated working for her brother. She promised me that she wouldn't tell him and she really needed it – he wouldn't provide one and I was the only person who could and she really needed the job so I did it and she told him that I had given her a reference (I didn't know) and when he asked me directly if I had I said 'NO'. I had sleepless nights and had to tell him – it was burning a hole in my heart and it was all I could think about. He understood but the look on his face told me everything. Never lied since. As soon as a lie rolls out the trust is broken forever and the feeling of remorse never goes. Not for me anyway.

What is your greatest achievement?

Staying the course when it all gets too much.

Tell me a secret about you:

I had a one night stand – unusual because you can count on one hand how many men I have slept with and still have fingers left. He was a gorgeous Rugby Player and I was at a night club with my sister, Ann. He approached me and I couldn't believe it!!! She was the one who usually got the attention. She saw that he was interested in me and came over and read him the riot act about her little sister. She said ' He's Ok, he's kind', so I took him back to my place and we had the most amazing, outrageous SEX. Afterwards he asked me to call him a taxi – I did and he said Bye – that was amazing!. I saw him out and glanced at myself in the mirror – I blushed and went to bed to enjoy the best night sleep ever. No, I have never seen or heard from him since!

If you could go back in time to age 20 with your current life experience, what would you do differently?

Go to Uni – have 5 kids - spend endless amounts of quality time with my mum.

There is a 15 year old standing in front of you. What life advice would you give him/her?

Don't sweat the small stuff. It really doesn't matter a fig!

When you are an elderly person, sitting in your rocking chair and you look back on your life, what do you want to have achieved?

The ability to rest without guilt. To enjoy the day because I have the time and not because I have the time off!

Give me one word that sums up your life journey thus far: Self-Motivated

What is the meaning of life?

To love and be kind and to nurture. To Love yourself and be kind to yourself and nurture yourself.

Thanks for the opportunity – that was therapeutic and recalling the one night stand was enjoyable!

Name: Sean Burn

Age: 35

Gender: Male (There are only two genders)

Country: South Africa (Living in England now)

Occupation: Web Developer

Do you believe in God?

I don't believe in God the way the term has been thrown about through the ages. Those who say you need to believe/have faith without proof of said "being" existing; just doesn't sit well with me. With that said, I do believe that there is some higher-power that keeps an eye on our tiny spec of cosmos dust from time to time, whether that can be construed as "God" well we will never truly know I guess. I don't "pray" in the sense; although I do have conversations with myself in places like the shower and give my point of view of what I really think about a situation, and if this "being" existed, then why the hell would it allow certain things to happen. (Most argue it's "Gods way of giving us free will", I call it bullshit.

If I could wake up one day and humanity had no idea what religion was, "Gods", Church etc, then I think this world would be a much better place. With that said, removing religion all together would be catastrophic if it were imposed by state powers.

We all need something to believe in, and I will admit that when someone I love or don't necessarily know is in peril, I will sometimes close my eyes at night and hope what is considered a prayer would be heard and answered. I guess it explains why death itself doesn't scare me, as I want to know what's on the other side.

If you're thinking all of the above is so contradictory and all over the place, then you now understand my point of view. Believing in God is a different experience for everyone.

What is the worst thing you've ever done?

Not taking my parents advice when I was a teenager, and thinking I "knew" best. As cliché as that may sound, not listening to them when they could clearly see all the danger signs, almost cost me my life. Running around thinking the world owes you; is not the way to live.

What is your greatest achievement?

Being able to accept that everyone is different, not everyone thinks the same, I can't change things I don't like about others and money can't fix stupid.

Tell me a secret about you:

I once masturbated to interracial lesbian midget porn while listening to Alan Jacksons' Album – Angels and Alcohol. It wasn't my proudest moment, but better than cheating on my long distance partner.

If you could go back in time to age 20 with your current life experience, what would you do differently?

As it stands I don't think I would want to go back in time and change anything; regardless of what I knew or could take back with me in terms of knowledge or experience. I am who I am because of what I have been through, experienced and done. These things have made me the man I am today, and I truly believe that "One often meets his destiny on the road he takes to avoid it" anyway. I've lived a pretty exciting and somewhat challenging life which has opened my eyes to many things, and going back with this knowledge would only make me live my early days being cynical and skeptical, rather than enjoying my life as I should be at age 20 and in my prime.

There is a 15 year old standing in front of you. What life advice would you give him/her?

1. As the expression of "respect is earned, not demanded" is as old as the hills, it does carry truth when it comes to your parents. Regardless of their societal standing, they would have seen and done things that they would move mountains to prevent you from repeating. Listen to them, take their advice, even if you think it's wrong, just keep it at the back of your mind and use it in your own way to tackle certain situations.

2. As you grow older you will learn that not everything you read is fact, and politicians are not your friends. Governments do not care about your well-being, and will do or say anything to get your vote. You will always be judged by the colour of your skin, and people who claim they do not see colour are liars and in denial. Blacks will be labeled as "opportunistic" with the "compensation culture" gene; all while being trapped in their own minds' prison to keep them from what they could achieve. Whites will carry this made up expression "white guilt" with them to make themselves feel better about past events they had no control over, or the actions of their forefathers; as well as to score brownie points on social media with their "progressive" friends.

3. Your heart will be broken many times, it will hurt; and each time you will think it's the end and you "have no reason to carry on"; this is not the case. Respect your partner, and never accept it when others tell you the "honeymoon" period ends eventually. It doesn't have to, and you don't need a celebrated calendar day just to send flowers or want to cuddle. Stand up for your partner, even if you know they are wrong; in front of others be a unified front and behind closed doors you can tackle them about it

4. Crying doesn't mean you're weak, it means you're human.

5. If someone tells you that "you can be anything you want" they're lying to you. Only a small percentage of the population can aspire to be anything they put their minds to, chances are you're average and will never be anything more than middle class. If you do

in fact become something great, create a legacy to be remembered by, then good on you and I'm the fool. But remember this, you only live as long as the last person who remembers you. That's not to say that you shouldn't aspire to do anything, as that's the only way you will learn your limitations and grow within. What you should be focusing on is your own happiness and not trying to please everyone around you.

When you are an elderly person, sitting in your rocking chair and you look back on your life, what do you want to have achieved?

I'm not afraid of dying, but I am afraid of dying alone. So my life goal, as simple as it is; would be to share my life "achievements" with someone. Regardless of what those "achievements" are, if you don't have anyone to share them with, then there's no point. It doesn't matter if I am rich or poor, the only thing that matters is that I do it honestly and with as little negative impact on those around me. I've spent too much of my life hurting loved ones, alienating myself and thinking the world "owed" me something. So when I'm sitting in that chair looking back, I want to be able to smile at the thought of knowing that I did everything in my power to make amends and do right by the people I wronged throughout my life because of my stubbornness. I would rather not be remembered than be remembered for being a horrible person.

Give me one word that sums up your life journey thus far: Conflicted

What is the meaning of life?

There is no one meaning of life. Life is what you do with it, and if life truly had one meaning then why would a 2 year old child who's got their entire life ahead of them, be diagnosed with leukaemia and be taken away without even a fighting chance? For those who are fortunate enough to live their lives, I believe are put on this earth to continue the species. That's it, nothing more, nothing less. Instead humans have become self-centered, "moral high ground" narcissists who only care about themselves. And yes this applies to every single person on this planet. At the end of the day the only thing anyone ever cares about is self-preservation, everything else is secondary. For anyone reading this who thinks I'm wrong or I'm an "asshole" because of my view; has just proven my point. Not everything is pretty roses and sunflowers. We have taken so much for granted as a species and it would take a catastrophic planetary reset by man or nature herself to align humans to thinking how we were created/evolved to. Instead we run around hurting each other, murdering out of greed and hatred and only thinking about ourselves and the life of "luxury" we could be living. Does that make me want to join some volunteer relief agency to make myself feel better into thinking I'm "making a difference? No it doesn't. It doesn't matter how much I think I'm doing to better society, the problems will never be eliminated; because humans are inherently selfish and we have reached the point of no return already.

Name: Suzanne Berkey

Age: 58

Gender: Female

Country: USA

Occupation: Office Manager

Do you believe in God?

Yes I definitely believe in God.

What is the worst thing you've ever done?

Unfortunately I am not going to share that, too ashamed. But God knows and he has forgiven me.

What is your greatest achievement?

Having my two boys.

Tell me a secret about you:

I have never got to ride in a limousine or ever been on a real vacation in my life.

If you could go back in time to age 20 with your current life experience, what would you do differently?

I would of went to college and became a doctor or lawyer.

There is a 15 year old standing in front of you. What life advice would you give him/her?

To trust In GOD. Never judge people. be kind to others, respect your elders and listen to them when they have something to say to you.

When you are an elderly person, sitting in your rocking chair and you look back on your life, what do you want to have achieved?

I want to be able to sit in that rocking chair knowing I have no doubt in where I will be when I die and to know I at least helped save one soul.

Give me one word that sums up your life journey thus far: Blessed

What is the meaning of life?

Life means to love, it means to hope, be thankful, but most of all the meaning of life is to do God's will. After all we are just a passing through this life to get to the everlasting side. So excited and can't hardly wait .

Peace, the gift of peace. I am thankful that I have that gift. Even in the heaviest of tears and heartache, and believe me I have has my share. I have a peace within my heart and soul that God is right there with me crying right along with me. He gives me inner strength always.

Name: Sébastien

Age: 45

Gender: Homme / Man

Country: France

Occupation: Directeur artisitique publicité / comédien / réalisateur

Do you believe in God? (en Francais and in English)

En Francais: J'ai cru en Dieu pendant longtemps – sans être pratiquant -. Et l'accident qui à emporter ma fiancé en 92, a atténué ce sentiment de protection. Aujourd'hui et avec le temps, mon sentiment profond est cet événement tragique et très douloureux a été une épreuve impose par... Dieu ou un dieu... enfin quelque chose bien au dessus de moi, pour que la vie d'après soit plus intense.

J'ai beaucoup de respect et un sentiment d'être dans du cotton – être en "pause" quand je suis dans les lieux réligieux – quelqu'ils soient – et en particulier, dans des églises.

In English: I believed in God for a long time – without practicing – . And then the fatal accident that happened to my fiancé in '92 mitigated that feeling of protection. Today, and over time, my gut feeling is this tragic and very painful event was an ordeal imposed by God or a god … … finally something right above me, for life after more intense. I have great respect and a sense of being in the cotton – be in " pause" when I'm in religious places – whatever they are – especially in churches.

What is the worst thing you've ever done?

En Francais: J'étais à Londres en stage et lors d'une soirée alcoolisée chez une des personne de l'agence – qui était fils de diplomate – dans son appartement très chic sur les bords de la Thames, j'étais tellement saoul que lorsque je suis allé aux toilettes pour le big stuff, j'ai aussi vomi de là où j'étais assi. Il y en avait partout et dans tous les sens. Mes habits étaient souillés. C'était le chaos. Ma plus grand honte. Surtout lorsqu'il a fallu demander de l'aide en anglais. On m'a douché, on a lavé mes habits. Bref le lost control total.

In English: I was on an internship in London and at a cocktail party with a person from the agency who was the son of a diplomat – in his chic apartment on the banks of the Thames. I was so drunk that when I went to the toilet for the big stuff, I also vomited where I was sat. It was everywhere and in every way. My clothes were soiled . It was chaos. My greatest shame. Especially when it came to asking for help in English. I was showered, my clothes were washed. In short I lost total control.

What is your greatest achievement?

En Francais: De transmettre à mes enfants ce que je pense avoir de bon en moi et d'être encore capable d'apprendre, d'être à l'écoute de la vie et des gens que je croise.

In English: To pass on to my children the good I think I have in me and still be able to learn, to listen to life and the people I meet.

Tell me a secret about you:

En Francais: Je crois qu'une bonne étoile m'accompagne. Je ne la vois pas , je ne l'entends pas. Je ne compte pas sur elle quand les choses ne vont pas bien mais quand tout a coup, les problèmes se dissipent par des manifestations inattendues (appel d'un ami perdu du vu, une proposition de travail alors je commencais à désespérer…), je me dis que j'ai de la chance d'être baigné par ce halo.

In English: I believe that good fortune is with me . I do not see, I do not hear it . I do not count on it when things are not going well but when suddenly problems are dissipated by unexpected events (call from a lost friend who'd seen a job offer when I was starting to despair …), I tell myself I 'm lucky to be bathed by the halo.

If you could go back in time to age 20 with your current life experience, what would you do differently?

En Francais: Je crois que j'aurais fait la meme chose! Suivre mon instinct, laisser parler ma créativité. J'ai eu la chance d'avoir la confiance de mes parents pour me laisser vivre mes défis, mes expériences.

In English: I think I would have done the same thing! Follow my instincts, let them speak my creativity. I was fortunate to have the confidence of my parents to let me live my challenges, my experiences.

There is a 15 year old standing in front of you. What life advice would you give him/her?

En Francais: Je lui dirais de me suivre , de lacher prise, pour fair e10 fois plus de choses que maintenant de ma faire entièrement confiance car la vie ne ferait que commencer.

In English: I would tell him to follow me, to let go , to make 10 times more things and now trust myself completely because only then, life would begin.

When you are an elderly person, sitting in your rocking chair and you look back on your life, what do you want to have achieved?

En Francais: Avoir pu donner du bonheur, un sourire , un moment suspendu aux gens que j'ai pu croisé meme que quelque minute et me dire que ce petit instant à changé leur vie en mieux pour tout le reste de leur vie ou l'espace d'une journée. Sans qu'il ne sache obligatoirement que je pourrais y être pour quelque chose.

In English: To have been able to give happiness , a smile, a moment suspended from the people I've crossed, even a few minutes and tell me that this little moment changed their lives for the better for the rest of their lives or a space in a day . Without them necessarily knowing that I am the reason.

Give me one word that sums up your life journey thus far: une chance – A chance.

What is the meaning of life?

En Francais: Les Monty Python ont répondus à ma place en regardant le coté le plus lumineux de la vie.

Mais le sens de la vie est surtout celui qu'on lui donne. Pour moi , bien que comme tout le monde, j'ai des hauts et des bas, la vie c'est de la joie chaque fois que le soleil se lève et aussi quand la lune prends le relais. La vie est un moment unique qu'il faut magnifié même par des choses qui peuvent paraitre insignifiantes.

In English: Monty Python answered my place watching the brightest side of life (Life of Brian)

But the meaning of life is especially that which we give it. For me though, like everyone, I have ups and downs, life is a joy every time the sun rises and also when the moon takes over. Life is a unique moment that must be magnified- even things that may seem insignificant.

En Francais: Je suis papa de 2 enfants. Voir la vie dans ses 1ere minute à l'air libre, c'est un privilège, une magie. Une partie du mystère dévoilé. Et je veux pouvoir faire des "tours de magie" à ceux qui m'entourent ou que je croise, chaque jours que la vie me prête.

In English: I'm a Dad to 2 children. Seeing life in its first minute in the open, it's a privilege, magic. Part of the mystery unveiled. And I want to make " magic " to those I meet around every day that lends me life.

Name: Sylvie Rutherford

Age: 61

Gender: Female

Country: France but now living in UK

Occupation: Tour Guide/ Tour Manager

Do you believe in God?

Sort of, but which one? Trying anyway but find it hard.

What is the worst thing you've ever done?

Kept money from Tuberculosis stamps given to sell when about 9/10 at school. I used the coins to buy sweets. Felt really, really bad and had to confess to my mother and after a lecture, she gave me the coins to give to school. Horrible memory.

What is your greatest achievement?

Suppose it is my boys.

Tell me a secret about you:

I was picked up when 15 to be an actress by a big cinema producer in Honfleur but my parents refused!

If you could go back in time to age 20 with your current life experience, what would you do differently?

Never ever be married. Horrible Contract. Stay free of choices all the time.

There is a 15 year old standing in front of you. What life advice would you give him/her?

Have a loved carrier and not depend on a man.

When you are an elderly person, sitting in your rocking chair and you look back on your life, what do you want to have achieved?

I would love to have been useful to people and animals, I would love to know I have given to others.

Give me one word that sums up your life journey thus far: Unconventional

What is the meaning of life?

I wish I knew. Just breed and die like everything else in Mother Nature. No meaning.

I think Art and Love and Dreams are the best things in life.

Name: Simon Harrison

Age: 53

Gender: Male

Country: England

Occupation: Company Director

Do you believe in God?

No - But a superior race of beings.

What is the worst thing you've ever done?

Smacked my son when he was about five.

What is your greatest achievement?

Had two beautiful children.

Tell me a secret about you:

I sometimes distort the truth with my wife so as not to worry her.

If you could go back in time to age 20 with your current life experience, what would you do differently?

Put my children through private school education and bought property.

There is a 15 year old standing in front of you. What life advice would you give him/her?

Never give up. Anything and everything is possible if you want it enough.

When you are an elderly person, sitting in your rocking chair and you look back on your life, what do you want to have achieved?

To leave my children and grandchildren secure.

Give me one word that sums up your life journey thus far: Interesting

What is the meaning of life?

The existence of an individual human being or animal.

Name: Miss Behaved
Age: 57
Gender: Female
Country: England
Occupation: Busy

Do you believe in God?

In hours of need, yes. In general I don't believe there's an ultimate god, an omnipotent presence. I believe in mother nature. I look around and see daily the wonders of this world that are awe inspiring - then I look at people and if we are made of God then God is not a very nice person. I lost faith because when I needed the comfort of my church and community it wasn't there. I thought that God was forgiving and there for everybody but it seems that God is only there when you are useful. I was ill and nobody was there for me. I was told by the vicar that, "Not all relationships can be nurturing." I find nature more forgiving because it's able to regenerate and renew.

What is the worst thing you've ever done?

Smacking my child because I was angry at something he'd done.

What is your greatest achievement?

My children are my first thought, and the fine men they've turned out to be. Also learning to learn with vision loss and functioning in my environment.

Tell me a secret about you:

Well, when I was younger my friend and I went into the church, dressed up in the vicars robes , rang the church bells - calling the faithful to service - and do you know what? No F****r came! Just shows the arid wastelands of faith on the estate we lived in. As we left we took all of what we thought were money envelopes stacked at the back of church only to find they were gift aid envelopes and empty. However, I'd like to add, in my adult life I did go on to become the church warden of our local Anglo-Catholic church, and a much respected one at that!

If you could go back in time to age 20 with your current life experience, what would you do differently?

I wouldn't buy cheap because you buy twice. I'd keep out of the sun because dealing with skin cancer 37 years later hasn't been pleasant. I wouldn't run for a bus and do an 8 hour shift in 6 inch heels because now my feet are knackered. I would question everything and not take things at face value and learn to be self reliant on an early age. Don't rely on anybody.

There is a 15 year old standing in front of you. What life advice would you give him/her?

"This too shall pass", which has been a mantra through all my life. Nothing bad or good will last forever. Don't be a sheep - don't follow the the crowd. And the above to my 20 year old self. You will never be as young and as beautiful as you are today which will apply to every single day of your life. Dreams can come true- I met Donny Osmond! But don't spend your life dreaming. Find a hobby you can do on a bus.

When you are an elderly person, sitting in your rocking chair and you look back on your life, what do you want to have achieved?

To have been loved and to have mattered to people and be remembered. I will have been happy to have left a beautiful rose garden I planted myself to whoever chooses to take a quiet moment and sit there.

Give me one word that sums up your life journey thus far: Challenging

What is the meaning of life?

I would think we are here once and for a short time- whether we matter is irrelevant or that important; its the impact I make on others and in this fragile world and looking after the environment. I try to reduce the food miles by growing my own. I was just about to say, we should enjoy our god given gifts but then thought about the first question and how I went full circle. Life is good - which I say everyday, despite my challenges. I feel very fortunate to be living in the UK and to not be predated by tigers, funnel spiders or snakes that can kill us.

What a time to be alive, good and bad.

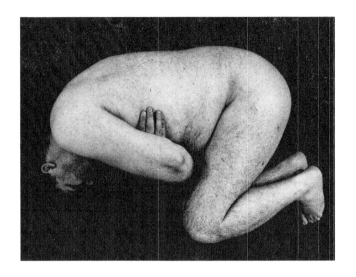

Name: Simon Lawrence

Age: 50

Gender: Male

Country: Great Britain

Occupation: Unemployed or "Fighter of a mental illness"

Do you believe in God?

If you are referring to a single identity that looks over us, created us in their image and grants us pardon when we sin and we thank when things feel right or good, NO. Is there a God or Gods, who knows, how can you tell and if so by what criteria and how would you prove or measure it? Are we all Gods, after all why does there have to be a single superior beginning, who is God?

What is the worst thing you've ever done?

Told the doctors to stop resuscitating my mother who was terminally ill with a brain tumour. It was her wish passed on in the briefest of moments and upon which I acted in equally of briefest of moments, whilst it was the right thing to do it felt so wrong. Who was I to say that was the moment mum was ready to pass away?

What is your greatest achievement?

To make someone smile and laugh, it is the most intoxicating experience I have yet to person too.

Tell me a secret about you:

This is something I have not shared with anyone before, it does not bother or trouble me to share it now. I once wondered what it would be like to have sex with another man and still cannot reason why it is such a social cancer and a defining matter in deciding ones place in the so called social standing. It has been an experience not at the sole discretion of humans.

If you could go back in time to age 20 with your current life experience, what would you do differently?

Now there is a question and one I can answer with ease. I picked up a camera age 20 and found something that I felt comfort and relaxed doing for the very first time. Sadly a very short while later I got married and started a family which consumed my life for the next 20 years and did not allow me to continue with my newly discovered passion. In short I would not get married or have a family but follow my heart and discover how far my photographic journey would have taken me.

There is a 15 year old standing in front of you. What life advice would you give him/her?

Never let go of the ability to laugh or appreciate laughter, no matter what circumstances or where you find yourself always carry a pocket full of laughter with you. A little to my mum's dismay the last thing I shared with my dad right before he passed away as a joke about the £5 he owned mum. It is very hard not to feel bad about something when you are laughing and if those around you don't get it they soon will or it is their loss. Laughter is one of the best forms of medicine I know.

When you are an elderly person, sitting in your rocking chair and you look back on your life, what do you want to h0ave achieved?

I do not need to become elderly or have a rocking chair to know that I have already achieved what I want. I have wanted and will continue to want to make someone smile every day. Even on the darkest of days I have been able to make someone smile and there is no better feeling than seeing a smile. It maybe tucked up behind a sourer puss face, but the eyes cannot hide a smile.

Give me one word that sums up your life journey thus far: Wondrous

What is the meaning of life?

It is a DVD on my bookshelf that sticks two fingers up at most of what we know about life(sorry could not help myself).Well writing the answers to these questions has become part of my life and therefore a sum of the it's total meaning so far. I am not sure I can reason or have the capacity to answer this question completely, that is if there is a complete answer. One meaning of life is quoted as *"being the condition that distinguishes animals and plants from inorganic matter, including the capacity for growth, reproduction, functional activity, and continual change preceding death."* So that excludes inorganic objects, objects that hugely influence and dictate our very lives, sometimes long before we are even conceived? To a fairly large proportion of the Earths human population existing day to day would not be possible without objects such as computers, the internet, mobile phones and even social media. The very idea of not being able to ask Google a question is, to many frankly life treating and beyond imagination or their ability to cope. We are, more than ever dependant things that we cannot readily control, we exist day to day and it is impossible for us to live any other way now. Well that is not entirely true, but it would require a breakdown in the social order and a step change in the way we live. Whilst I respect, to a point, where a large proportion of humans has got to in terms of technology and evolution I do feel that the group is slowly but surely taking steps backwards regarding skills like basic understanding (especially emotional), communication and respect. I won't be seeing that happen in my time and in some respects that makes me feel sad. We can imagine beyond our current limits with colour, depth and passion, yet I feel that we are neglecting our roots and losing control of that ability. Ignorance on the level we demonstrate is not a healthy thing, pushing problems around on any scale so we do not have to resolve them short term is not healthy. Douglas Adams was spot on the money when he described the *"Somebody Else's Problem"* field in his Hitch Hikers Guide to the Galaxy series.

As I have said I do not think I will ever experience what I believe to be the true meaning of life within humanity, even regarding those close to me. I see it every day in the animals and insects that go about their lives as I sit in my garden or the nearest field despite our best efforts in hindering their path. I do take some comfort, all be it a romantic one, in knowing that one day the Earth will be rid of us human beginnings and that the scars we have inflicted will heal.

Name: Tracy

Age: 46

Gender: Female

Country: United States

Occupation: Writer, artist, maker

Do you believe in God?

I believe in the universe and nature. The idea of God, has become to me, our attempt to personify the things which we don't understand, as a way to try to explain the universe to ourselves. Not only that, but as humans, we like to look outside of ourselves for answers or solutions to our problems. I feel that when we do that, we lose something along the way. The universe and nature are wondrous enough for me. When I am pondering a problem for a solution, the simple act of getting out into nature and connecting with it, and myself, is so powerful that I feel no need for anything more than that.

What is the worst thing you've ever done?

The worst thing I've ever done is to have relinquished my power to others. What I mean by that, is that I spent many years being what others have expected of me. Not only that, I've spent much of my life allowing others entirely too much input on my decision making process. Thank goodness I am still young enough to live the rest of my life differently.

What is your greatest achievement?

My greatest achievement has been to learn to walk my own path in life, with the understanding that not only is it my right to pursue my own dreams and happiness, it is my responsibility. It hasn't been easy getting here, but to finally understand that taking care of myself and standing up for what I feel to be right is not the same as selfishness.

Tell me a secret about you:

After a brief time about twenty years ago, lasting about a year, as an environmental activist, I've been quietly getting more involved in certain environmental and social causes. It feels good to be re-connecting with my early roots, and I look forward to getting back into the swing of things, doing what I can to help bring awareness and action where it's needed. This is among the things I was thinking about when I answered the question about the worst thing I've ever done, because it is one of the things which is a part of my core being, and in the past I allowed others too much of a role in my decision making process, even stopping my involvement with the things which matter greatly to me in order to placate others. Thank goodness that phase of my life is over!

If you could go back in time to age 20 with your current life experience, what would you do differently?

I would do exactly what I'm doing now. Sure, my life would have been different had I stayed the course, but I'm just grateful that I'm doing what I'm doing now. Having the life experience that I have is an added bonus in many ways.

There is a 15 year old standing in front of you. What life advice would you give him/her?

To live their life as fully as possible, and to pave their own path. As long as what they are doing isn't harmful to themselves or others, I feel that young people should be encouraged to assume as much responsibility for making their own decisions as possible. This is how they gain a sense of themselves and grow to be truly independent and free.

When you are an elderly person, sitting in your rocking chair and you look back on your life, what do you want to have achieved?

I want to have mastered the art of living joyfully and with love, while being strong and independent.

Give me one word that sums up your life journey thus far: Empowering

What is the meaning of life?

To learn to appreciate the beauty of life itself and to make the most of our time here. This means pursuing happiness, living with love, and finding ways to make the world a better place. This doesn't mean martyrdom. It is quite the opposite, because when we find ways to pursue or own passions and joy, we are much more equipped and capable of enriching the lives of those we meet. It's all about striking a balance.

By understanding how connected we all are to other people and the universe itself, it becomes more clear that it is important to be mindful of our impact. It is important however, to remember that our best contributions to the world are those which we make while living a life true to ourselves, doing the things which give us a sense of happiness and fulfilment.

Name: Steve

Age: 35

Gender: Male

Country: United States of America

Occupation: Police /Fire /EMS

Do you believe in God?

Yes. I was baptized as a teenager. My relationship with God grew distant over the years of my early adulthood. From time to time, I came back to my faith, but drifted away. Over the past year, I have gone back to my faith and have formed a closer relationship with God than I have ever had before.

What is the worst thing you've ever done?

I knew from an early age that my calling was to serve the public. Ever since a young child, I wanted to be a police officer and firefighter. Knowing that, I lived a pretty straight forward life throughout my teenage and early adult years. Yes, I committed some traffic violations while driving, but I never committed any serious crimes. I would have to say that the worst thing I've ever done would be sins of the flesh.

What is your greatest achievement?

My greatest achievement has been in obtaining a great career. I have the career of my dreams. I have been granted with the opportunities to obtaining training and experience to get me to the position of my dreams. I was lucky enough to achieve this at the young age of 24. While there have certainly been ups and downs since then, I am still proudly serving in the career of my dreams.

Tell me a secret about you:

A secret about me is that I am self-conscious. While I am very outgoing in my career, I am not outgoing in my personal life. An example of this would be my physical fitness, or lack thereof. I have always been a bigger guy. While I have tried and am trying to get into the best shape as possible, I am still a stocky guy. Because of this, I have rarely attempted to pursue a relationship with someone because I have felt that I wasn't good enough for them because I wasn't physically fit.

If you could go back in time to age 20 with your current life experience, what would you do differently?

While I am happy with a lot of details about my life, there are things that I would do differently. I stopped attending college after earning an Associate's degree (two year degree) to start my career. If I had this to do over, I would continue throughout the full four years and earn a Bachelor's degree before starting my career. I would be more socially outgoing. I wouldn't be so shy and self-conscious. I would actively pursue relationships and friendships.

I would form a strong spiritual relationship much earlier in my life.

I would spend more time with family.

There is a 15 year old standing in front of you. What life advice would you give him/her?

Get in church, find your faith, and keep your faith
Don't doubt yourself and/or put yourself down
Dream big and chase your dreams
Always put your family before your career
Never stop learning

When you are an elderly person, sitting in your rocking chair and you look back on your life, what do you want to have achieved?

I want to have positively touched lives.

I want my life to have been a success. I want to have the love of family and friends (hopefully a wife and children) I want to have a strong faith that I am very passionate about.

Give me one word that sums up your life journey thus far: Challenge

What is the meaning of life?

To live and love. To serve a loving God. To serve others.

One of the things about my life that I am most proud of is the fact that I have achieved nearly every goal that I have ever set. Some of the goals were easily achieved. Others required work and dedication. Some were achieved when people told me it couldn't be done. Other goals are still yet to be achieved, but are under steady work.

Name: Urs

Age: 43

Gender: Female

Country: UK

Occupation: Civil servant.

Do you believe in God?

No. I can't believe in anything that's used as an excuse for killing and war. Religion is responsible for too much wrongdoing in this world.

What is the worst thing you've ever done?

I regret some bad relationship choices; and I've handled a few situations very badly. I'm ashamed of an episode back in the late 90's when I was quite vile to a complete stranger in Newcastle. If I could find that woman now and apologise to her, I would.

What is your greatest achievement?

Becoming an aunt to two beautiful and clever girls, even though it required no effort on my part. Becoming a solo homeowner and getting promoted were also huge achievements for me.

Tell me a secret about you:

Erm, no.

If you could go back in time to age 20 with your current life experience, what would you do differently?

I'd be more steadfast in my beliefs and decisions, and would take less crap from other people.

There is a 15 year old standing in front of you. What life advice would you give him/her?

Listen to your Mum's advice, even if you decide not to follow it; she's generally right about most things.

When you are an elderly person, sitting in your rocking chair and you look back on your life, what do you want to have achieved?

To have had a fulfilling and loving lifetime with my family and dearest friends.

Give me one word that sums up your life journey thus far: Safe

What is the meaning of life?

It's better to share one's time than one's money. Money doesn't buy happiness, but quality time with people can.

Name: Terry Irving

Age: 66

Gender: Cis-Male

Country: USA

Occupation: Scrounger

Do you believe in God?

No.

What is the worst thing you've ever done?

Slept with a friend and former lover in order to break a long fast after my divorce. It wasn't forced but it was pressured. I apologized about 25 years later. She hasn't spoken to me before or since. It wasn't violent or evil but it was wrong. It didn't fit with who I thought I was.

What is your greatest achievement?

Surviving.

My mother was a drunk and my father, an enabler. When I was born, my mother left the house for a long time—six or eight weeks, I never got the full story—and, after she died (from cirrhosis of the liver, of course) I found notes she'd written about the fact she couldn't find it in herself to love me. I received two things from my parents: no love or false love from my mother and almost no support after I was 19 years old. Oh, and a genetic propensity to clinical depression. I also had what R.D.Laing called "knots." (I couldn't say that my mother didn't love me because my mother said she loved me and she was my mother so she wouldn't lie but I knew she didn't love me.)

The only way to survive sane was to stop loving my mother so I did at about 18 and never spent another 24 hours under her roof. I found out she was a drunk when I was about 30. I didn't like her when she was alive and I didn't like her when she died. She was in absolute misery for about a week and I stood there one afternoon and thought that if I really loved her, I'd put a pillow over her face and end her pain. But I didn't love her and so I let her live in agony for another week. Don't miss her or my father. It's the only advantage of having alcoholic parents.

So I paid for my own final year in college working three jobs, got along with no money in my first jobs, got ahead for a couple of years and then, in September 1984 when I was 32, put one kid into college with my retirement savings, my wife had a baby, and I bought a house. Haven't had a dime since but I've put another kid through college, supported both for years, paid all my bills, got thrown out of my home so my wife could try another guy, got re-married in 2000 to a girl I met in 1973, supported my second daughter and son-in-law through ten years of college and then the Great Recession, bought another home I couldn't afford and lived in it quite happily for 15 years, have only taken two vacations in my life when I wasn't worried about money every day, and found myself completely without savings at 65 years old. Paid for a lot of awards with a massive burnout caused by depression (the awards were caused by depression as well, funny that.) One daughter hasn't spoken to me in 8 years after I told her she was an alcoholic, the other turned into a wonderful mother and daughter (who tends to win arguments by simply saying, "Oh you're just being crazy, Dad") I do have a wonderful wife, great grandkids, and a dog who is a delight. I still can't go on vacation without worrying about money every moment.

Tell me a secret about you:

Jesus, weren't there enough in the preceding paragraphs? I guess it's not a secret but I don't believe that anything I do is done well enough—from raising children to writing books. It's a shame that my depression is clearly genetic and due to some fuckup with my brain chemicals because I'd love to blame my mother. Oh, and I never figured out War Reporting. I put my crew in danger over and over again because I couldn't see the dangers in front of me.

If you could go back in time to age 20 with your current life experience, what would you do differently?

Go to Law School and get a job in Finance. I don't go to my college reunions now because it's one of the best colleges in the nation and more than half the grads are already retired with millions. I'm driving an Uber to survive. I might have still gone into journalism AFTER Law School but it would have been nice to make some real dough first. I have a friend who comes from wealth and married wealth. He went into private banking, then law school, and now races 30-foot yachts across the South China Sea and has an apartment on Central Park South. He didn't do as well in college as I did so I don't think he's smarter.

There is a 15 year old standing in front of you. What life advice would you give him/her?

Go to Law School or something else that is socially useless but financially rewarding. Don't do anything you don't enjoy every day. Look for a job that you wake up and want to go to. Take adventures when you can because you can never go back later.

When you are an elderly person, sitting in your rocking chair and you look back on your life, what do you want to have achieved?

I would like to have really given a shot at being a racing driver. I took a course and was told I was really good but then, children, money, houses…it all vanished. I can still remember every foot of every turn of the crappy little race course in Connecticut.

Give me one word that sums up your life journey thus far: Survival

What is the meaning of life?

Take care of those entrusted to your care without thought of yourself. Love what you do if you can.

A short attention span is a wonderful thing. Sure, if something great happens to me, I usually lose the euphoria in a matter of minutes but something terrible (or that my diseased brain believes is terrible) disappears just as quickly. After that, it's usually just putting one foot in front of the other. Dum-de-dum-dum.

In a very true and deep sense, I never expected to live this long.

I had a life that even amazed me. Hitched across the country twice, slept under cars and on the open beach, hired lear jets and crews on my own decisions, got shot at but they missed (to quote Churchill), conquered every tough job I was faced with until about 50 when Bloomberg all night put me down, saw Hong Kong, Thailand, El Salvador, South Africa, Beirut, France, England, the fall of the Berlin Wall. Was loved by one wonderful woman and slept with far more than I ever expected. Managed to do it without cheating or breaking my word. Survived on my own and made my own choices. Didn't succeed every time, but a majority of the time. Took care of my families at the cost of my own comfort Remember standing in Fort Lee, NJ and realizing that I was completely on my own, had no money to support my family, no one who would bail me out if I failed at this particular program— strange feeling. Wrote a book, found an agent, found a publisher who LOVED the book, went to market. I got to see the damn book with the professional cover and my name on it. Then the publisher went out of business and it all disappeared. Edited/rewrote a second book—a labor of love that took up three years without pay—which was and is a wonderful intelligent, loving, honest portrayal of war. (Tony Hirashiki is going to be awarded the Asian American Journalists Lifetime Achievement Award in July. It's a secret).

Name: The Late Phoenix

Age: Forgot, been ages since I slurped birthday cake

Gender: Fluid but male

Country: Citizen of the world and mostly universe

Occupation: Broke thinker

Do you believe in God?

There can't be any separation, right? for those poor souls whom God banishes to Hell. If God is Everything God is Hell also. What other substance would you be made out if not for God? That would allow you to be separated from God

What is the worst thing you've ever done?

Not seen Don's Plum sooner. Can't believe I wasn't invited to the screening, this is a great underground B&W low-budget piece of independent filmmaking featuring some up-and-comers before they were famous. It was filmed in the very Don's Plum Van Nuys location directly in front of the street I grew up on as a kid. Never forget the neighborhood. You never forget your childhood diner and bar.

What is your greatest achievement?

The A-Z thing I did last year.

Tell me a secret about you:

I can't talk. But I can sing. I can only sing.

If you could go back in time to age 20 with your current life experience, what would you do differently?

Go to art school. come up with Regular Show first. Change my name to Mordecai.

There is a 15 year old standing in front of you. What life advice would you give him/her?

Run,

When you are an elderly person, sitting in your rocking chair and you look back on your life, what do you want to have achieved?

Wait I actually built a rocking chair? that's my singular life achievement right there, I am not handy at all. I'm a philosopher not a practicalizer. If you give me house paint and a brush I'll use the brush for my moustache and huff the paint.

Give me one word that sums up your life journey thus far: NIN

What is the meaning of life?

The meaning of life is to find the meaning of life, that's finally the correct answer, right?

On the scrounge for that love the preacher was talking about…

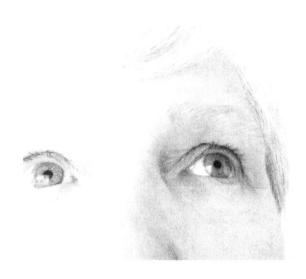

Name: Val

Age: 59

Gender: Female.

Country: UK

Occupation: Psychotherapist

Do you believe in God?

Not sure, would like to as I envy those with a strong faith howovor, I havc too many quesliuiis.

What is the worst thing you've ever done?

I stole some money off of my Aunt when I was a teenager, only 2 shillings but had a huge impact, shame and guilt as she had been my refuge during a very difficult childhood. As an adult I confessed to her and apologised.

What is your greatest achievement?

Having my 3 children who I love more than life itself.

Tell me a secret about you:

I would not marry the man I lived with for 20 years, he was not good for me, kept me in victim role. This is hard for me to admit as it would mean I would not have my children, but maybe I would have me a lot earlier.

If you could go back in time to age 20 with your current life experience, what would you do differently?

I would not have married my husband, he was a bully and kept me in victim…this is hard for me to admit as I would not have had my children who I love more than anything.

There is a 15 year old standing in front of you. What life advice would you give him/her?

Just to grab all opportunities, push yourself past your comfort zone to be the best you can be.

When you are an elderly person, sitting in your rocking chair and you look back on your life, what do you want to have achieved?

I want to have made a difference in people's life, I want my life to have meant something more than just procreation.

Give me one word that sums up your life journey thus far: Challenge

What is the meaning of life?

I don't know. My meaning is to give to others what I wish to have for myself. I need to make my life worthwhile, to make a difference.

Name: Tom Massie

Age: Forbidden…just kidding…58

Gender: Male

Country: United States of America

Occupation: Security Officer, although I cling to my past as a Ferrier, horseman, and a cowboy. I had been working with horses, in one capacity or another, for 35 years prior to a severe injury placing me in a job I could rehabilitate in-security. Be careful what you ask God for but be thankful when He keeps His promises.

My memories are filled with unimagined accomplishments, witness to amazing wonders that His creation could provide. From a calving season marking the beginning of the cowboy's year of life; renewed by the calves bouncing innocence through newly greened pastures, to deaths own beauty in the golden leaves of the Aspen trees in the fall as elk burst out into meadows between the groves. Of the smells of a horse as you saddle up and begin a day before the sun rises. Feeling as if you were the only two sharing this special time with God prayer of thanks escaping your lips. The bond growing with your horse as your work partner and to God for providing a moment that won't go unforgotten.

Looking out onto to a field of fresh snow that no one has spoiled. The absolute quiet it creates, muffling everything. Appreciating its purity.

Reminiscing can be enjoyable and painful at the same time.

I shouldn't make it seem that I am not grateful about my job as a security officer. I was injured one day while moving cows on a step slope in Wyoming. Long story short, my back and hip were in bad shape. I was unable to work effectively for a few weeks. I came to realize it could be longer than that if I didn't receive some therapy. I moved to Texas where God provided me with a job that keeps me mobile and healthy and with a place to live. I believe He did this in answer to a prayer uttered a few days before the accident, and a heart attack to boot.

Do you believe in God?

Without question! Yes! More and more every day. I was saved when I was 14 years old and have known that God is very real since I was old enough to remember.

My memories were filled with go to church with friends before my parents decided to start going back to church when I turned ten years old. I would feel the love found there, people would be nice and I wouldn't have to worry about ridicule. I am no saint mind you. I found myself rodeoing and in doing so began to run with a less than saintly herd of cowboys. I have also compromised my values here and there through life to achieve my self-centered desires. Each time I managed to destroy a bit of myself, the parts that counted the most, along with hurting others also. I began to carry regrets, the sort that always are there to whisper in your ear as you began to do the right things. 'You aren't worthy, look at what you have done. Who wants a failure in life like you? God will never be able to use a sinner like you'. For a while it worked, I even doubted my own salvation.

Each time I have allowed myself to step back toward that pit of self-misery, He has been there to pull me back. I often jest about God having to use a two by four on me to get my attention. This is in fact truer than not. Never underestimate Grace. God keeps His part of the bargain whether we choose to or not.

God became to me who He always was, my Savior, willing to forgive the unforgivable. Me.

He has been the One constant source of real love in which to turn to as the world has become a colder place to be, apart from Him.

What is the worst thing you've ever done?

If I were to go to the true source of all my lengthy list of 'worst things', I would find the times when they began is when I chose to stifle God's voice and do what I wanted. The worst thing I have done was to act like I loved someone when I did not. Imagine the irony of this. I did this to a woman I knew cared for me and I was lonely.

At the same time, I would have had to turn my back on God's love, my relationship with Him in order to have done such a heinous act to her.

What is your greatest achievement?

Becoming a father, then being one.

Tell me a secret about you?

Won't that mean it is no longer a secret? I have vivid dreams of my future, they often come true.

If you could go back in time to age 20 with your current life experience what would you do differently?

I would be tempted to correct the mistakes I had made, naturally. Mostly, I would be brave when I needed to be and wasn't. Shut my mouth when I should of, listened to others wisdom and used it. Loved others more honestly. Sacrificed the stupid things I thought were important for the lasting ones that do.

Loved myself in a way that allowed me to be honest and sincere about who I was and trust.

Would have pursued God and chosen to have gone to a theological college.

I would have stayed in the horse world somehow because it provided insight into God's love and creation like none other.

A thousand times I allowed myself to imagine the what ifs of this scenario. The answers come easy, but one. Would I do as much with that gift of a second chance if I had to forfeit the gift of grace and forgiveness for things the way they are now.

There is a 15-year-old standing in front of you. What life advice would you give him/her?

The skeptic says, not sure the kid would listen. The heart would say, look at what is important to achieve a happy life. When you decide on a work you want to do in life, look at those who have gone before you and see where it has led them. If that's what you deem worthy than pursue it.

If you want to value yourself, be willing to serve others first. Be that person to others that you want them to be to you. You are not alone in this world and love is worth every moment of the work it takes, whether easy or tough. You won't find satisfaction in life if you can't love yourself first, so do what you know is right and that way you will never have to hang your head before anyone. Speak the truth, be courageous in your convictions. Be kind when others are not. Do the unexpected because it is the right thing to do. Never tire from doing good. Find your worth in your actions, not in others opinion of others. Make each day count, because they do. Your words count either for good or harm, use them wisely and with true intent, even in your humor. Pursue truth, for it will lead you to God's grace and love.

When you are an elderly person, sitting in your rocking chair and you look back on your life, what do you want to have achieved?

Being satisfied with who I am. Knowing that I did my best in following my values. Being loved by family and friends. Having truly loved someone who truly loved me. Being an example to the world of the love that Jesus had for me. To have not only asked God to forgive me of my sins, but to have allowed that grace to extend to abolishing my regrets. To have held the hand of a love every day I can. To never lose the smell of a horse in my mind, the beauties I have seen and not have shared these things with others.

To not have taken for granted the life I have been given.

Give me one word that sums up your life journey thus far. Unanchored

What is the meaning of life?

Pursuing God's love while living here as He intended. Balancing that life in remaining faithful to yourself with the values that will carry you through. Responding to others in love and using the gifts we have been given in those pursuits.

I have often wondered how I would answer questions like these, if I would honestly or not. I suppose there would be things said or thoughts acknowledged if others could not see it. I save these for my conversations with the One who understands it all, who forgives it all, who rejoices with me in my greatest moments. My heart longs every day to share the special things in life. That may very well be my deepest secret. That I still believe in love.

Thank you for asking.

Name: Anniesu of Runswick

Age: 50

Gender: Female

Country: UK

Occupation: Therapist

Do you believe in God?

I reject the concept of God as sold to us in the Western world. It is masculine, punitive and diminishing of the feminine, creative, nurturing aspect. When I look at the world and what has been done in the name of religion over the centuries all I see is pain, destruction and separation. Why would I accept that?

I follow a Pagan spirituality. In the Pagan tradition the connectedness of all life is acknowledged and celebrated. We celebrate the turning of the wheel, the changing seasons which each bring their own gift: the new life of spring, the abundance of summer, the harvest of autumn and the restfulness of the winter months. Each season can be seen as a metaphor for life.

What is the worst thing you've ever done?

I don't regret anything that I've done in my life, everything was done with the best motive at the time. However, I feel very sad that I couldn't be with my dear friend Rob when he died as I had told him that I would be.

What is your greatest achievement?

Without a doubt my three sons.

Tell me a secret about you:

As I get older I find myself becoming more bisexual in my attractions.

If you could go back in time to age 20 with your current life experience, what would you do differently?

Left my abusive marriage earlier and followed my heart more!

There is a 15 year old standing in front of you. What life advice would you give him/her?

Don't take yourself too seriously. Life isn't just about chasing material things, they're not the things that you carry with you as you get older!

When you are an elderly person, sitting in your rocking chair and you look back on your life, what do you want to have achieved?

When I was 30 I found out that I was pregnant with you youngest son. I phoned my parents who were living abroad at the time to give them the news. My Dad's response was to ask me what I was going to do with my life. As I put the phone down I thought, 'If I raise three reasonably well adjusted children, then I will have done something with my life.' I've done that. Everything else is a bonus!

Give me one word that sums up your life journey thus far: Growthful

What is the meaning of life?

Joy! Taking time to enjoy the space in between: those moments when life isn't happening.

Name: Timmy Tiger

Age: 45

Gender: Male

Country: UK

Occupation: Engineer.

Do you believe in God?

Yes-ish, not a disbeliever, but don't attend church either…suppose I'm one of those who'd pray in times of dire straits / grief.

What is the worst thing you've ever done?

Not buying a house before prices shot up!! And not returning the park pedalo within the hour and insisting I'd only been out for 40 mins to save paying more !!!

That's not the worse thing you've ever done though is it?

No – it's not…

What is your greatest achievement?

Travelling around the world independently for nearly 3 years with self made adventures such as walking Mount Everest base, working in ski chalet over ski season …too many adventures to list !

Completing an Ironman in 11 hours.

Competing for Great Britain in duathlon for my age group.

Tell me a secret about you:

I went wrong walking up Mount Everest trek…added another 5 hours onto the day and nearly collapsed with exhaustion in the middle of nowhere!

If you could go back in time to age 20 with your current life experience, what would you do differently?

I'd do a degree in sports science and work in the research / sport industry…and buy a couple of houses. But am quite happy with my travels / adventures, so wouldn't change that much.

There is a 15 year old standing in front of you. What life advice would you give him/her?

Carpe Diem. Don't do tomorrow what you can do today -grab every opportunity and find time to talk to everyone, whatever age they are.

When you are an elderly person, sitting in your rocking chair and you look back on your life, what do you want to have achieved?

Firstly, not to fall out of the chair looking back. Secondly, a head full of happy memories and laughs.

Give me one word that sums up your life journey thus far: Free-spirit

What is the meaning of life?

A DVD in the 'M' section at HMV!

The Analysis

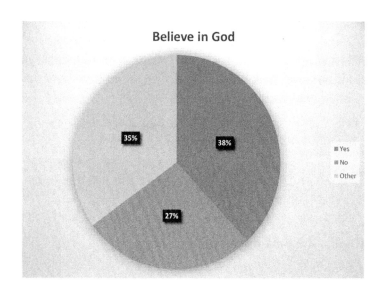

Believe in God

35% | 38% | 27%

Yes
No
Other

Do You Believe in God?

- 73% of all people had faith - 38% had faith in God and 35% in something else. A high percentage of the hundred people questioned have hope and believe in something spiritual.

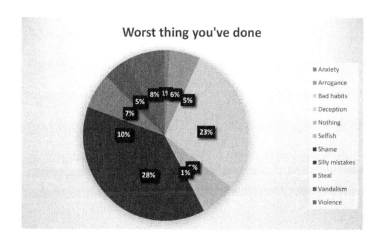

Worst thing you've done

- Anxiety
- Arrogance
- Bad habits
- Deception
- Nothing
- Selfish
- Shame
- Silly mistakes
- Steal
- Vandalism
- Violence

What is the worst thing you have ever done?

- Shame and deceit were the main things that held people back in life as the worst thing they had done. It's usually that which makes us feel guilty that impedes us,

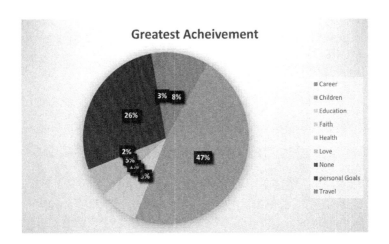

Greatest Acheivement

Legend:
- Career
- Children
- Education
- Faith
- Health
- Love
- None
- personal Goals
- Travel

Values shown: 3%, 8%, 26%, 2%, 5%, 47%, 3%

What is your greatest achievement?

- 48% of people said that having children was the most important thing they had done followed by 26% achieving set personal goals.

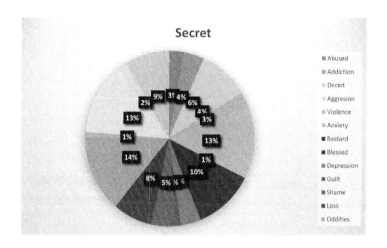

Tell me a secret about you:

- What a mixed bag of secrets we keep! We all have our skeletons.

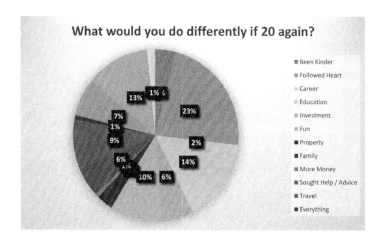

What would you do differently if 20 again?

- Been Kinder
- Followed Heart
- Career
- Education
- Investment
- Fun
- Property
- Family
- More Money
- Sought Help / Advice
- Travel
- Everything

If you could go back in time to age 20 with your current life experience, what would you do differently?

- 23% of people said if they could go back they would follow their heart followed by 14% saying they would have worked harder and 10% would have had more fun.

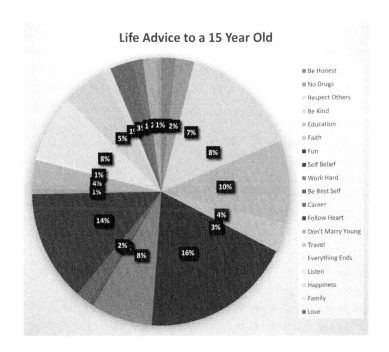

Life Advice to a 15 Year Old

Legend:
- Be Honest
- No Drugs
- Respect Others
- Be Kind
- Education
- Faith
- Fun
- Self Belief
- Work Hard
- Be Best Self
- Career
- Follow Heart
- Don't Marry Young
- Travel
- Everything Ends
- Listen
- Happiness
- Family
- Love

There is a 15 year old standing in front of you. What life advice would you give him or her?

- Advice to a young person had 16% saying you should have self-belief, 14% go and follow your heart and 10% for getting a good education.

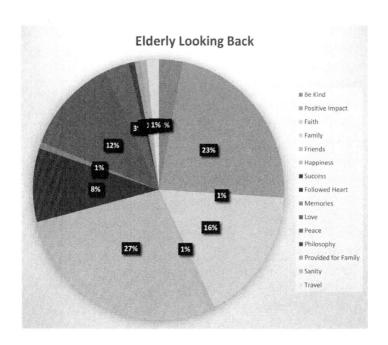

Elderly Looking Back

Legend:
- Be Kind
- Positive Impact
- Faith
- Family
- Friends
- Happiness
- Success
- Followed Heart
- Memories
- Love
- Peace
- Philosophy
- Provided for Family
- Sanity
- Travel

When you are an elderly person, sitting in your rocking chair and you look back on your life, what do you want to have achieved?

- Looking back over life when elderly had 27% wanting to see happiness, 23% leaving a positive impact and 16% having had a family.

The Meaning of Life

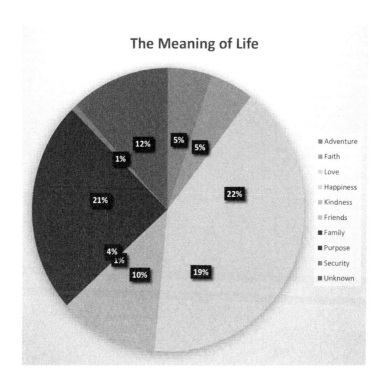

Legend:
- Adventure
- Faith
- Love
- Happiness
- Kindness
- Friends
- Family
- Purpose
- Security
- Unknown

Values shown: 12%, 5%, 5%, 1%, 21%, 22%, 4%, 1%, 10%, 19%

What is "The Meaning of Life"?

Based on the culmination of answers to this final question 72% of people agreed that love, purpose, happiness and kindness are the meaning to life.

Along that journey it would appear that having faith, following your heart, and self-belief were key elements. Listening to your elders, getting a good education and working hard to achieve your goals. Build a loving family, be kind, and leave a positive impact. However, don't forget to have fun along the way.

I hope that this wonderful collaboration has given a clear and constructive answer to the meaning of life and will be your go-to book whenever you need some good, honest life advice!

Now, my dear reader, it's your turn.